Plays for Puppet Performance

GEORGE MERTEN

Plays for Puppet Performance

George Merten

Publishers   PLAYS, INC.   Boston

Copyright © 1979 by PLAYS, INC.

All rights reserved.

Portions of the material in this book previously appeared in EIGHT PLAYS FOR THE PUPPET THEATRE by George and Elizabeth Merten and in THE HAND PUPPETS by George Merten.

Library of Congress Cataloging in Publication Data

Merten, George.
    Plays for puppet performance.

    CONTENTS: Introduction. — The king's dinner. — All change for spring. — Spider's eye view. — [etc.]
    1. Puppets and puppet-plays. [1. Puppets and puppet-plays]
I. Merten, Elizabeth, joint author. II. Title.
PN1980.M47   812'.5'4   79-4512
ISBN 0-8238-0234-5

Introduction

Puppetry has a very long tradition as a theatrical medium, and there is some evidence that it predates the live theatre. One of the fascinations of puppetry is that it combines many of the arts — sculpture, painting, design and, above all, theatre.

The live actor must "assume" on stage a particular role in a manner that will be convincing to the audience. The puppeteer, on the other hand, creates the character and so, unlike the live actor, who has to recreate the part he plays for every performance, the puppet remains in character at all times. It is this single identity, sustained through the use of voice and movement, that makes a well-designed and well-constructed puppet character believable and convincing to the audience.

This most important aspect is often overlooked when puppeteers produce a play. The attention of an audience cannot be guaranteed simply by holding up a puppet and making it move. Whether you have had considerable experience or are embarking upon your first production, you must prepare and rehearse your performance: There are no shortcuts.

Begin by reading the play several times, until you feel you know it thoroughly. Then try telling the story to someone, without using the script. Study his reaction. Does the story hold his attention? Have you succeeded in evoking his interest? If not, is your interpretation at fault? Have you chosen a play that you are not ready for, or are you insufficiently prepared? The play must have meaning for you if it is going to have meaning for your audience.

The preparation outlined above is essential before you begin designing the production. In reading the play you will have undoubtedly built up a mental image of your characters — their physical appearance, their personalities, and some of their individual quirks. Never begin construction of a puppet until you know exactly what you expect from it in the performance of the play. A production should be designed as a whole. Don't start making the individual puppets until you have understood and established the necessary relationships between them so that you will successfully convey the play's meaning to your audience.

If the production is a group effort, all members should be involved in the preparation. Only after everyone has a full understanding of the play and the director's intent should the individual talents within a group be utilized in the construction of the characters, sets, costumes and properties.

While such an approach to a production may seem overly time-consuming, it will prove to be the exact opposite in the long run. The first thoughts of the producer and performers should not be, how easily can I do this, how little rehearsal can I get by with, but rather, how much work does it require? Can we use some puppets we already have? (This may indeed be possible in some instances, but be sure you are not doing it out of laziness.) If you have the right attitude, you will give to the puppet play the same exacting attention that is necessary for a live play.

Once the puppets and the other essentials are ready, rehearsals can begin. At this point the director must take full charge of the production. This does not imply dictatorship, but rather that whatever suggestions group members make during rehearsals (and these should not be discouraged), the director must make the final decision. Any changes must conform to the concept of the play already developed by the director — otherwise an uneven production will result.

Rehearsal necessarily involves a great deal of repetition that can result in monotony and consequent loss of vitality in the play itself. To avoid this, vary the rehearsals as much as possible by working on scenes and individual bits of "business." Don't go slavishly through the entire script at every rehearsal. If you have difficulty in establishing a particular mood at any point, playing a piece of music may assist you to capture or recapture the mood.

These days the script is usually recorded on tape, but don't feel that the recording you begin rehearsing with must be the final version: You may find you have "business" that the tape does not allow time for, or that the voice inflection is unsuitable for a movement you feel necessary for your interpretation. If so, re-record sections as necessary.

The most critical aspect of rehearsal is the manipulation of the puppets — the movement that largely carries the play. Good manipulation comes only with practice and a "feel" that is partly an extension of your own empathy with the character and partly the empathy emanating from the puppet itself.

Manipulation should be planned but not stilted; no movement should be without meaning. Complete absence of movement at given moments can be overwhelmingly expressive, provided the "pose" has meaning. The worst and, unfortunately, the most persistent misconception regarding manipulation is that the puppet must at all times be moving when speaking so that the audience will know which character is saying the lines. This, of course, is nonsense and is more likely to irritate than enlighten. Usually, "compulsive" movement takes the form of jiggling the puppet, but this conveys nothing of the meaning of the words. Puppets obviously have limits to their range of possible movements. Jiggling a puppet will use up all possible movements in a few seconds. Economy of movement is the essential factor.

One way to help convey meaning and, incidentally, to improve manipulation is to mime the story. This means, of course, that all participants in the production must be thoroughly conversant with the play, since they will not have the support of the words. In mime only deliberate movement should be used, or the meaning will be lost. Discipline is the key to mime and to good manipulation.

Discipline is part control and part concentration, not only upon what you are doing with your puppet, but also on what the other characters are saying and doing. This involved having your puppet visibly attentive to the lines and actions of the others on stage and reacting to them. Nothing is less convincing than an obvious lack of rapport between actors who are supposedly involved in the same situation. Achieving a plausible rapport entails good manipulation and your own constant personal receptiveness to the total situation, since the puppet is, after all, an extension of yourself. It is doubly important, therefore, to ensure that the tape you are working with enables you to act and react in the most effective manner. It will help to make all the work you have put into the production worthwhile.

* * *

Elizabeth Merten, who wrote five of the plays in this volume, was a musician and writer. She was long associated with His Master's Voice Company and frequently wrote for *The Gramaphone*, England's leading magazine on recorded music. Before settling in Canada, she performed with puppets on B.B.C. television and then became a regular performer on the Canadian Broadcasting Corporation network. She also wrote and narrated many music programs for children for C.B.C. radio. Music was always an integral part for her own distinctive puppet productions.

— **George Merten**

The King's Dinner

a one act play for hand puppets by Elizabeth Merten

Characters

MR. JAMPOT	a fat cook
MR. BEANPOLE	a thin cook
KNAVE OF HEARTS	a boy
LANCELOT	a lion

Properties   A plate of tarts; a bottle of wine; a big sheet of white blanket cloth or foam rubber.

Scene   A kitchen in the palace of the King of Hearts. At extreme stage-left a cooking-stove with pots and pans; at left centre stage a kitchen-table; at right centre stage the flap of a trap-door attached by hinges to the back of the playboard.

Production notes

This play is designed for a children's audience of mixed ages.

It is quite straightforward and should present no particular problems. There are plenty of opportunities for action.

The voices of BEANPOLE and JAMPOT, in particular, should be well defined since they have to alternate quickly in conversation when they are bickering.

LANCELOT, the lion, should, of course, be costumed, because he has a speaking part. This makes the character more convincing and also heightens the fantasy.

The main properties are the stove, table and trap-door. These should all be placed in the positions suggested, otherwise they will prove to be obstructions to the free movement of the puppets.

The stove and the table should both be low built, otherwise, when they are standing on the playboard they will mask too much of the puppets.

The trap-door should be hinged to the top edge of the playboard so that it falls flat on the playboard when it is thrown open. A pin hinge will probably be found to be

1

the most satisfactory means of hinging the flap to the playboard. In this way the flap can be removed from the playboard when other plays are given in the same programme. Only one side of the hinge remains screwed to the edge of the board and this should not cause any inconvenience.

The only other property that requires consideration here is the large piece of rolled-out pastry that Beanpole and Jampot throw over Lancelot. This could be a piece of heavy, cream-coloured cloth, or blanket material, but perhaps a sheet of thin foam rubber would be more effective. It would also be the right colour and could provide some action if the two cooks were to handle it and stretch it before using it to capture the lion. Care should be taken that the rubber sheeting is thin enough to wrap around Lancelot without tending to spring away.

The plates of tarts should be so constructed that the Knave of Hearts can pick them up and disappear with them quickly.

The bottle of wine could be shaped out of wood. A piece of lead let into the bottom would enable it to be placed on the table with less chance of it being toppled over during the action.

The King's Dinner

[*As the curtain opens, the two cooks are busy by the stove.*]

JAMPOT: Did you put salt on the potatoes, Beanpole? [*Beanpole puts his nose in the air and doesn't answer.*] Did you or didn't you?

BEANPOLE: I won't answer — I'm insulted. [*Knave enters from stage right.*]

JAMPOT: Here comes that nuisance again.

KNAVE: Compliments of the King of Hearts to the Chief Cook . . . . .

BOTH COOKS: [*alternately*] That's me . . . that's me . . . no, it's not . . . yes, it is . . . no, it's not . . . yes, it is . . .

KNAVE: Quiet, please. His Majesty would like to know what's for dinner.

JAMPOT: Pot-roast . . .

BEANPOLE: Boiled potatoes . . .

JAMPOT: Carrots . . .

BEANPOLE: A nice, green salad . . .

BOTH COOKS: And chocolate pudding for dessert.

KNAVE: Oh? Chocolate pudding? Who thought of that?

BOTH COOKS: [*alternately*] It's my idea . . . no, it's not . . . yes, it is . . . no, it's not . . .

KNAVE: Well, it really doesn't matter anyway because the King wants tarts for dessert.

BOTH COOKS: [*alternately*] This is too much! Not again! I can't stand it! I shall refuse to do it!

KNAVE: Some of Mr. Jampot's raspberry ones.

JAMPOT: [*crowing over Beanpole*] Huh! I knew he liked mine best.

KNAVE: And some of Mr. Beanpole's lemon ones.

BEANPOLE: Huh! So there!

KNAVE: And don't forget a bottle of cherry wine to go with them, at seven sharp. [*Knave exits right.*]

BEANPOLE: Oh, go away, Knave!

JAMPOT: I'll seven sharp him one of these days!

BEANPOLE: Well, who's going down in the cellar to get the wine?

JAMPOT: It's your turn.

BEANPOLE: It is not.

JAMPOT: [*exploding*] It's not, it's not, it's not! That's all I ever hear from you! What with that and baking tarts, tarts, tarts every day of the week, I'm going crazy!

BEANPOLE: Why, my dear Jampot, I'd no idea you . . . . .

JAMPOT: I feel like taking off my cap and apron and walking straight out of here forever.

BEANPOLE: But that's how *I* feel too!

JAMPOT: A pleasant change — for once we're agreed about something.

BEANPOLE: Well, I'm sorry if I upset you.

3

JAMPOT: I'm sorry too.

BEANPOLE: Now you have a little rest and I'll fetch the wine.

JAMPOT: No, I shouldn't have asked you . . . it was my turn . . . I'll go . . .

BEANPOLE: But I'd like to . . .

JAMPOT: No, I insist . . .

BEANPOLE: So do I insist . . . [*pause*] . . . Oh dear, there we go again.

JAMPOT: Very well then, Beanpole, you go down to the cellar and I'll get the tarts out.

BEANPOLE: Good — that solves it. I thank you, Jampot. [*He lifts the trap-door and descends, closing the door behind him. Jampot exits stage left, comes back with a plateful of tarts and places them at right-hand end of table.*]

JAMPOT: [*as he returns*] I do wish the King would have something else for dessert once in a while. It's really getting on my nerves. My, that pot-roast smells good. [*He turns and goes to stove. Knave steals in behind his back and takes away the plate of tarts. Beanpole comes up from below, bringing a bottle of wine, sets it on the table, closes the flap down.*]

BEANPOLE: [*as he emerges*] Ah-tish-oo! Ah-tish-oo! Oh goodness, I nearly dropped it.

JAMPOT: [*not looking round*] Nasty cold you've got, Beanpole.

BEANPOLE: [*as he closes the flap*] No, it's that dusty old cellar that makes me sneeze. Don't forget the tarts, will you?

JAMPOT: [*not looking round*] There they are on the table.

BEANPOLE: Where? I don't see them.

JAMPOT: [*turning round*] Right there on the t . . . . . Beanpole, what have you done with them?

BEANPOLE: Me?

JAMPOT: Now I warn you . . . I'm not in the mood for silly jokes.

BEANPOLE: I like that! I didn't even see them and there you go blaming me again!

JAMPOT: There's no need to get excited. Calm down.

BEANPOLE: Calm down yourself. You just forgot them, that's all.

JAMPOT: I'll prove to you that I didn't. Now then, how many platefuls of tarts did we have in the pantry half-an-hour ago?

BEANPOLE: Two.

JAMPOT: Are you sure of that?

BEANPOLE: Positively.

JAMPOT: Well, if I brought out one plateful, then there's only one more plateful left, isn't there?

BEANPOLE: I suppose so.

JAMPOT: Wait a minute and I'll show you. I'll take the wine and put it on the ice at the same time.

4

BEANPOLE: [*as Jampot goes off with the bottle and returns with another plateful of tarts*] I still don't see how we could just lose a plate of tarts . . . I mean, it couldn't disappear into thin air!

JAMPOT: This is the last plateful, so that proves it. [*He puts it on the table.*]

BEANPOLE: Are you sure?

JAMPOT: Come and see for yourself. [*They both go off stage left and the Knave comes up through the trap-door, takes the plate off the table and takes it below, leaving the door open.*]

BEANPOLE: [*as they return*] You were right, Jampot, and it's a good thing we've still got . . . we've still . . . [*pauses and stares at table*] . . . look!

JAMPOT: Oh no, it's impossible!

BEANPOLE: Look, the cellar door's open!

JAMPOT: Go down, Beanpole! There must be somebody down there . . . quick, quick! [*Beanpole goes down, pushed from above by Jampot.*]

BEANPOLE: [*voice getting muffled as he descends*] Stop, thief, stop thief! Where are you? What have you done with our tarts?

JAMPOT: [*calling down*] Catch him, Beanpole . . . have you got him . . . hang on to him . . . just wait till I get my hands on him!

BEANPOLE: [*coming up gasping*] Not a sign of anyone . . . all I found was one poor little lemon tart with a bite out of it on the floor.

JAMPOT: The brute! But wait a minute . . . that's a clue, don't you see?

BEANPOLE: How could a tart be a clue?

JAMPOT: The next person who comes in here with sticky hands will be the thief.

BEANPOLE: Oh, you are clever, Jampot.

JAMPOT: I've a good idea who it will be, too.

BEANPOLE: Oh, do we have a suspect already?

JAMPOT: You wait and see — but the first thing is to get some more tarts baked right away. [*He goes off stage left and returns with a large roll of white cloth or rubber, looking like a roll of pastry-dough.*]

BEANPOLE: [*while Jampot is out*] Fancy dropping one of my tarts on the dirty floor . . . there's no excuse for that, none at all.

JAMPOT: Give me a hand to roll this out, will you? Good thing I had some dough prepared for the next batch, wasn't it? [*A sneeze is heard from below.*]

BEANPOLE: What was that? Listen! [*Another sneeze.*] He must be coming back for more! What shall we do, Jampot?

JAMPOT: This time he'll get more than he bargained for. Here, quick, take one end of this and stand over there on the other side of the door.

BEANPOLE: You mean we're going to catch him with the dough?

JAMPOT: Yes. Sh-sh, here he comes! [*The lion's head comes up and they smother him in the dough, push him down on the floor and hold him down. They cannot see who they have caught. The muffled roars of a lion come from inside the dough.*]

JAMPOT: Got you!

BEANPOLE: Oh, my goodness, isn't he strong? Just listen to him! Oh, Jampot, I hope we've caught the right person!

JAMPOT [*laughing and spanking the bundle*]: Ho! Ho! Don't make so much noise — we're not afraid. We know it's you, Mr. Seven Sharp.

BEANPOLE: Mr. Seven Sharp! But that's what you call the Knave of Hearts!

JAMPOT: [*laughing again*] The very same, but not so sharp now, eh? [*He begins to spank the bundle in time with the following words.*] The Knave of Hearts, who stole the tarts and took them clear away. [*More roars from the bundle.*]

BEANPOLE: Oh, Jampot, don't you think it sounds more like a lion? . . . Look, here's a tail too. O-h-h-h, I'm scared!

JAMPOT: A tail, did you say? Don't be silly, that's impossible.

BEANPOLE: But here it is! Oh, Jampot, what have we done? [*They move back in alarm and the lion shakes off the dough and raises himself up.*]

BOTH COOKS: O-O-O-O-H! [*They cling together, trembling visibly.*]

JAMPOT: Save me, Beanpole!

LANCELOT: Will someone please tell me what's going on here? Who are you?

BEANPOLE: I'm . . . B-B-B-Beanpole.

JAMPOT: I'm . . . J-J-J-Jampot.

LANCELOT: Don't be afraid, gentlemen. I'm sorry I made such a noise just now but I couldn't breathe in there. You gave me an awful fright, you know.

BEANPOLE: Oh, Mr. Lion, we . . . we . . .

LANCELOT: Lancelot's the name.

BEANPOLE: L-l-l-Lancelot, we're very, very sorry. We thought you were someone else.

LANCELOT: So I gather.

JAMPOT: We thought you were the thief who stole our tarts.

LANCELOT: Oh, I see. Well, I'm just a tourist. You know it's visiting day at the palace, when your King kindly allows visitors to walk in and look around. I wanted to do the whole palace from top to bottom and when I found myself in a dusty wine-cellar with some wooden steps at one end I couldn't resist climbing up . . . and here we are.

JAMPOT: I hope we didn't hurt you, Lancelot.

LANCELOT: Oh, I'm fine — a little dazed but still curious. Tell me more about this thief of yours.

BEANPOLE: Well, we think it's the Knave of Hearts. He's the King's page-boy and he delivers orders to us here in the kitchen in a most impertinent way.

LANCELOT: And helps himself to your goodies, does he?

6

JAMPOT: We suspect him, Lancelot, and we'd like to teach him a lesson he won't forget.

LANCELOT: Let me see now. I'd like to help you. What if I were to borrow a cap and apron and pretend to be a cook . . . how would that . . .

BEANPOLE: Oh, that certainly would give him a shock . . . I'm afraid he's not a bit scared of us.

JAMPOT: The very thing, a wonderful idea.

BEANPOLE: But you wouldn't hurt him, would you?

LANCELOT: Dear me, no, I won't hurt a hair of his greedy little head. Just lend me some things to wear and leave it to me.

BEANPOLE: Come along to my room, then, and I'll find you a cap and apron. [*As they move off to stage right, Jampot calls after them.*]

JAMPOT: Beanpole, would you please throw the dough in the garbage as you pass by? We can't very well use it now.

LANCELOT: Allow me! [*He helps to remove it and he and Beanpole exit.*]

JAMPOT: [*to himself*] But we still haven't any tarts for the King's dinner and no time left to bake any now. Seems to me there's nothing else we can do but send up the chocolate pudding and hope for the best. I'd better go and see if *that's* still there. [*He goes out to stage left and returns.*] Yes, I must say it looks delicious.

BEANPOLE: [*re-entering from stage right*] Lancelot thinks you and I should hide in the pantry when the Knave comes back and keep our ears to the keyhole. He's just putting on the cap now. Are you ready, Lancelot?

LANCELOT: [*re-entering from stage right in cook's cap and apron*] How do I look, friends?

JAMPOT: H'm, more like a lion than a cook, I'm afraid, but if you could keep your back turned over there by the stove, it might work all right.

LANCELOT: That's what I shall do.

BEANPOLE: We'd better get out of the way, Jampot. Hurry, I think I hear him coming. [*They scurry off stage left as Lancelot goes to stove and bends over it.*]

KNAVE: [*entering from stage right*] It's nearly dinner-time, Mr. Jampot. Is everything ready? [*No answer.*] Mr. Jampot, you're not sulking again, are you? [*No answer.*] What a sulky cookie you are! Wouldn't you like to know what I call you and Mr. Beanpole behind your backs? [*No answer.*] If you don't answer me, I'll pull your apron-strings! [*He creeps up behind Lancelot and, as he touches the back of the apron, Lancelot turns round quickly and growls.*]

LANCELOT: Gr-r-r-r-r!

KNAVE: [*in a state of shock and panic*] O-o-h! Help! Help!

LANCELOT: [*fiercely*] Stand still, boy! [*Knave stops running round and stands trembling, until Lancelot gets near him.*]

KNAVE: Oh-oh-oh! [*hastily moving away again.*]

LANCELOT: I said stand still . . . That's better . . . now hold out your hands. [*He bends his head over to sniff them.*]

KNAVE: Oh, don't eat me, please!

LANCELOT: Sticky hands . . . why?

KNAVE: I d-d-d-don't know.

LANCELOT: You do know! Gr-r-r-r!

KNAVE: [*hastily*] Oh, all right, then — it must be from eating tarts.

LANCELOT: And where did you get the tarts?

KNAVE: I d-d-don't know.

LANCELOT: Gr-r-r-r-r! [*He comes closer.*]

KNAVE: [*hastily and in a high voice*] I stole them.

LANCELOT: A-a-h!

BEANPOLE: [*rushing out*] Ah-hah!

JAMPOT: [*rushing out*] Ah-hah!

KNAVE: [*dismayed*] Oh-oh!

BEANPOLE: You rascal!

JAMPOT: You rogue!

KNAVE: I won't do it again, I promise. Where did that lion come from? I thought he must have eaten you up!

LANCELOT: We're not all like you, Knave — we don't think about eating all of the time! How are you going to punish him — that's the next thing.

KNAVE: Oh dear, I think I'll go now. [*He tries to escape but Lancelot stops him.*] Ow! Let me go!

JAMPOT: His punishment will be to tell the King the true reason why he can't have tarts for dinner tonight.

LANCELOT: Very good, very good.

KNAVE: But he doesn't WANT tarts for dinner tonight!

BEANPOLE AND JAMPOT: Wha-a-a-t?

KNAVE: No, I'm the one that wants them all the time.

BEANPOLE: Do you mean that His Majesty would like something else for dessert?

KNAVE: Yes, he would. Only today he said to the Queen: "I suppose we'll be having those wretched tarts again tonight". Hah! Hah! Hah! [*laughs*]

BEANPOLE: [*very upset*] Wretched! My beautiful tarts!

JAMPOT: Never mind, Beanpole — it's the best news I've heard for a long time. Just think of it — we don't need to bake any more for at least a year! Hurray, hurray!

BEANPOLE: [*joining in*] Hurray, hurray . . . come on, Jampot, let's go and put some whipped cream on the pudding. [*They go off together laughing.*]

8

LANCELOT: Well, no more tarts for *you*, my boy — that looks like your real punishment.

KNAVE: Don't tell them, please, but I like chocolate pudding nearly as much!

LANCELOT: [*laughing*] Oh, what a boy you are!

KNAVE: [*laughing too*] Oh, what a lion *you* are! [*They slap each other on the back and go on laughing, as the curtains close.*]

All Change for Spring

a one act play for marionettes by George Merten

Characters

MRS. RABBIT	a kind motherly rabbit who hates to see anyone unhappy.
MR. SQUIRREL	very agreeable, but likes to show off at times.
CLARENCE	an unhappy caterpillar because he is the only one in the forest who has not yet become a butterfly.
SAMMY SKUNK	in this instance an agreeable character.
A BIRD	
TWO BUTTERFLIES	these are on one control.
LARGE BUTTERFLY	this is Clarence after the metamorphosis.

Properties   a large rock
a log

Scene   A clearing in the forest, surrounded by trees and other foliage. A fairly large rock is at left centre stage. There is room to pass behind it. A log should be lying on the ground in the clearing.

Production notes

As a general principle, it is more effective to costume animal characters when they have a speaking part. It makes the character more believable and heightens the fantasy. They should, where possible, stand upright.

The scene for this play is set in a clearing in the forest. It will be effective to have the wing tabs designed into the uneven edges of bushes or trees.

The important property in the setting is the rock behind which the Caterpillar eventually retires. This should be large enough to conceal effectively both the butterfly (which is there from the beginning of the play) and also the Caterpillar. It will probably be found more convenient to make a cut-out rock and suggest the texture with paint. Mount this on a flat board, reaching towards the back of the stage, and make sure the rock will not topple forward. A lamp can be mounted on the board that will glow in the closing stages of the play when Clarence becomes a butterfly.

In the casting of the voices, care should be taken that each voice is well defined in character. It too often happens that voices used in animal plays have a tendency to sound somewhat similar. This, of course, makes identification of the characters difficult.

The CATERPILLAR can be made from a length of soft window shade spring, covered with soft brown fur, or other suitable material that will not offer great resistance. A small piece of lead should be inserted in both ends of the Caterpillar. Two strings are attached, one at the head and one at the tail. The head can be modelled on. The eyes are the prominent feature.

The control is a single wooden bar, slightly longer than the Caterpillar. A string should also be attached to the centre of the body and passed through a hole in the middle of the control bar. This string controls the arching of the body. A curtain ring should be tied to the end of this string, above the hole, to prevent the string slipping back through, and also to act as a control by which the string is manipulated.

MRS. RABBIT would look well with large, upstanding ears and a hat sitting between them. She is obviously a motherly type and is quite worried by the Caterpillar's unhappiness.

MR. SQUIRREL could be dressed in pants and a loose fitting jacket. SAMMY SKUNK should wear only pants in order to show off his white stripe.

In both cases, the tails can protrude through the back of the pants.

All three BUTTERFLIES can be made of doubled tarleton or buckram. The wings should be cut out in one piece and glued in the centre underneath short wooden bodies. Markings can be painted on the wings. A small piece of lead should be fixed to the underside of the bodies to give control.

Strings should be attached to both ends of each of the butterflies' bodies.

The two butterflies can be gang-strung on a single long control bar, but care should be taken that they are sufficiently separated, so that they do not come too close together in flight and become entangled with each other. A slight shaking of the control will cause the wings to flutter.

The BIRD should be large enough to allow adequate control of its movements.

The beak need not have a controlled movement, but a slot or small hook, will be necessary to hold the string from which the notice is suspended. It would be well to letter the "Do Not Disturb" sign on both sides of the board.

Due to its size, the wings of the bird will have to be flapped by manipulation from the control. Leather provides effective hinging for bird's wings.

The lighting will be even throughout the play.

All Change for Spring

[*When the curtain opens Mrs. Rabbit hops in from stage left, followed by Mr. Squirrel. They are full of fun and good spirits and hop and run about while chattering cheerfully.*]

MRS. RABBIT: My, Mr. Squirrel, what a beautiful day it is! It is really good to be alive!

MR. SQUIRREL: Yes, Mrs. Rabbit, everyone seems to be so happy just now. Why, I saw Sammy Skunk chatting with some of the flowers this morning. He was admiring their perfume.

MRS. RABBIT: Wasn't that nice of him. Were they nice to him, too?

MR. SQUIRREL: Oh, yes, they were saying the loveliest things about his beautiful white stripe. It is strange what an effect weather has on us, isn't it, Mrs. Rabbit?

MRS. RABBIT: Yes, it really is strange.

MR. SQUIRREL: [*taking a deep breath*] If it were always like this everybody would be too happy to want to quarrel with anybody else. [*Two butterflies come in stage right and fly around for a few seconds before flying up and out of sight.*] What a wonderful world we would have. Just look at those butterflies. Aren't they beautiful!

MRS. RABBIT: They have so much energy, but, of course, they do not have very long to use it up, do they?

MR. SQUIRREL: At least they don't have to put up with the winter.

MRS. RABBIT: I wonder what it would be like to fly?

MR. SQUIRREL: Perhaps they wonder what it is like to hop and run.

MRS. RABBIT: It is strange isn't it, how we all do things so differently and — what was that! [*A quiet sobbing is heard off stage. It gets louder.*] Gracious me! It sounds like someone crying, but who could be unhappy on a day like this? [*Both begin looking around for whoever is making the sound, but do not look stage right.*]

MR. SQUIRREL: I can't see anybody.

MRS. RABBIT: Neither can I. I wonder who it can be? [*Caterpillar enters from stage right, arching his back and moving forward slowly, still making a sobbing sound. Mr. Squirrel suddenly sees the Caterpillar.*]

MR. SQUIRREL: Why, Mrs. Rabbit, it is Clarence Caterpillar. [*He moves across and bends down to Caterpillar.*] Clarence, why are you so unhappy? [*Mrs. Rabbit also bends down over Caterpillar.*]

MRS. RABBIT: Yes, Clarence, how can you be sad on a day like this? It is absolutely wonderful just to be alive. [*Caterpillar raises his front half from the floor and looks at Rabbit and Squirrel.*]

CLARENCE: But Mrs. Rabbit, I feel so ashamed.

MRS. RABBIT: Ashamed! Whatever have you to be ashamed of Clarence? You are always so quiet and never get in anybody's way. I can't see why you should be ashamed.

CLARENCE: Well, . . . well . . .

12

MR. SQUIRREL: You can tell us, Clarence. We feel so good to-day, we only want to help everybody. Isn't that right, Mrs. Rabbit?

MRS. RABBIT: Of course, Clarence, you just tell us and we'll help you.

CLARENCE: That is awfully good of you, Mrs. Rabbit, and you, too, Mr. Squirrel, but it isn't anything you can help me with. Nobody can help me. I'll just have to wait—

MR. SQUIRREL: [interrupting] Of course we can help you if you will only tell us what it is. It is no use waiting and being miserable.

CLARENCE: Oh, I feel so ashamed. [A cheerful humming is heard and Sammy Skunk comes merrily on from stage right. He jumps clumsily over the log and capers around.]

SAMMY: Why are you three just standing around on a day like this? Why, it's beautiful. Come on, let us play chase around the—

MR. SQUIRREL: Be quiet a minute, Sammy. Poor Clarence Caterpillar is unhappy about something.

MRS. RABBIT: And he says he is too ashamed to tell us what it is.

SAMMY: What can he have to be ashamed of? Come on, Clarence, tell us your troubles. Then we can start a game.

CLARENCE: Don't let me stop you playing. I'm sorry to be a nuisance. Just leave me alone and I suppose I shall be alright if I wait long enough.

MRS. RABBIT: But we can't be happy and play while you are so miserable, Clarence. You must tell us what it is.

CLARENCE: But, Mrs. Rabbit, even if I tell you, you can't help me. Please go and play and forget me.

SAMMY: Let's do that. If Clarence sees us playing, it might make him forget his troubles.

MR. SQUIRREL: Well, I suppose it is no good all of us being miserable. Let us see who can jump the highest.

SAMMY: You know you can — and Mrs. Rabbit can jump too, but I can't jump very high.

MR. SQUIRREL: Well, Mrs. Rabbit and I will jump and you can judge. Come on Mrs. Rabbit. [Squirrel begins jumping up in the air. Mrs. Rabbit follows suit and for about ten seconds they are jumping up and down and chattering. Finally they stop, a little out of breath.] Who won, Sammy? Who jumped the highest?

SAMMY: Why, you know you did! Let us play a game that we all have a chance to win.

MRS. RABBIT: Yes, I think that is fair, but I do wish Clarence would be happy too. [Clarence has retreated to stage right and isn't taking much interest in the game. He rises up occasionally and sways slowly from side to side.]

MR. SQUIRREL: What game shall we play? It is not easy to play with you, Sammy. You can't move fast enough.

SAMMY: We could play a game that uses our brains. Then I have as good a chance as you two. Even Clarence could play a game like that.

MRS. RABBIT: But he doesn't feel like playing. He is too miserable. Perhaps it is because he moves so slowly. You can at least run Sammy, even if it isn't very fast.

MR. SQUIRREL: What kind of a game can we play with our brains?

SAMMY: Well, we can ask riddles and things like that—

MR. SQUIRREL: We can do that on a rainy day. On a fine day like this, we should jump and play.

SAMMY: Then I had better go and find someone else to play with, and you and Mrs. Rabbit can jump and run all you like.

MRS. RABBIT: I don't really feel like running and jumping while Clarence is being miserable. I wonder what is wrong with him? [*The two butterflies swoop in again and fly around for a few seconds before going out again. Caterpillar stops moving and lies still. Squirrel jumps about again.*]

MR. SQUIRREL: I can jump alright but I wish I could fly sometimes.

MRS. RABBIT: Fly! Why that is ridiculous. How — oh! . . . Come here, Sammy Skunk and Mr. Squirrel. I have an idea. [*All three animals gather with their heads together and Mrs. Rabbit whispers to them. Occasionally one of them looks at Caterpillar to see if he has observed them, but he is not taking any notice. At the end of this they separate a little and look in the direction of the Caterpillar.*]

MR. SQUIRREL: Of course, that must be the trouble, and I really don't see how we *can* help him.

SAMMY: Should we tell him that we know his trouble?

MRS. RABBIT: I think that might upset him still more. Perhaps we can think of a way to make it easy for him to tell us. Then we can say that there is nothing to be ashamed of at all.

MR. SQUIRREL: What can we think of? You were talking about using brains just now, Sammy Skunk. What ideas have you got?

SAMMY: Well, we might say that it is nice to have a caterpillar with us and we hope he will stay.

MR. SQUIRREL: We could say that, perhaps, but he might guess why we were saying it.

MRS. RABBIT: We mustn't hurt his feelings, but I am sure he would feel better if he could talk to us about it.

MR. SQUIRREL: Let us ask him is he is feeling any better. You ask him, Mrs. Rabbit.

MRS. RABBIT: Yes, I will. [*Moves towards the Caterpillar.*] Clarence, we are thinking of a game to play. Have you any ideas?

CLARENCE: I really don't feel like games just now, Mrs. Rabbit.

MRS. RABBIT: It might take your mind off your troubles if you joined in our game. [*At this moment a large black-bird flies in from stage left, making a cackling sound.*]

14

SAMMY: Do you have to make all that noise?

BIRD: Just letting you know I am around. My, it's good to fly on a day like this. What! Is that a caterpillar I see over there? [*Flies over Clarence.*] Why, so it is. What is he doing here?

MRS. RABBIT, SAMMY AND MR. SQUIRREL: [*together*] S-s-sh! S-s-s-s-h-h!

MR. SQUIRREL: He is not very well.

BIRD: Not very well! I don't wonder at it.

CLARENCE: Oh dear, I do seem to be causing a lot of trouble. I think I had better tell you why I am unhappy, but I feel so ashamed.

BIRD: I hope I didn't say the wrong thing —

CLARENCE: Oh no, it wasn't your fault. Everybody would realize it sooner or later. I may as well tell you myself.

MRS. RABBIT: Now just take your time, Clarence.

CLARENCE: Well, the truth is — the truth is — I should have turned into a butterfly before this, but I haven't.

MRS. RABBIT: Oh dear! Well, never mind—

CLARENCE: But I think I am the only caterpillar left in the forest. All my friends are flying about and looking so pretty. You see, you can't help me, can you?

SAMMY: Perhaps the bird could take you for a ride and you could see what it is like.

BIRD: Yes, I'll be pleased to do that—

MRS. RABBIT: No, no, that would not be good at all.

MR. SQUIRREL: Perhaps it isn't warm enough?

SAMMY: Perhaps you aren't comfortable enough?

MRS. RABBIT: Well, I have never yet heard of a caterpillar that didn't turn into a butterfly. It is just a matter of waiting — it could happen any time.

CLARENCE: Thank you, Mrs. Rabbit. I suppose it will happen, but I don't like being the last one.

MR. SQUIRREL: Let us make up a nice cosy place for Clarence to change in. That will be as good as a game.

SAMMY: Yes, let's do that.

CLARENCE: That is very good of you but I don't think it is really necessary.

MRS. RABBIT: We would like to do that for you Clarence. Come along everybody. Let us make a comfortable place behind this rock. He will be private there. [*The Bird flies off stage left. The Rabbit, Skunk and Squirrel all busy themselves around and behind the rock. The Bird flies in with something soft, like cotton batting, in his beak and lets it fall behind the rock. He then flies off again. There is a general chattering going on. Clarence has moved nearer the scene of activity.*]

MRS. RABBIT: [*from behind rock*] There! I think that is going to be most comfortable.

15

MR. SQUIRREL: Now, Clarence, it is all ready for you. [*Caterpillar moves towards the rock while they all stand aside and watch.*]

MRS. RABBIT: Don't you feel happier now?

CLARENCE: I think I do and thank you very much for all your kindness. [*He rises up and begins to twitch.*] Perhaps it won't be long now. [*He continues to twitch.*]

MRS. RABBIT: Goodness, Clarence, are you all right? It seems as though something is happening to you.

SAMMY: Perhaps his wings are beginning to flutter.

CLARENCE: I do feel a little peculiar. I wonder if it is really going to happen now? I do hope so.

MRS. RABBIT: I think you had better go behind the rock, Clarence, just in case. [*Clarence is still twitching at intervals, but hurries behind the rock.*]

CLARENCE: [*from behind the rock*] Yes, I am sure something is happening. It is very nice here.

MR. SQUIRREL: We will wait for you. [*The Bird flies in again. This time he has a notice in his beak that says "Do Not Disturb." If possible, let it fly down and release the notice so that it leans against the front of the rock. If this is too difficult, let the bird hover just over and in front of the rock, retaining the notice in its beak. The animals are all waiting anxiously, wanting to look, but refraining from doing so.*]

SAMMY: Are you ready yet, Clarence?

CLARENCE: No, not yet.

MRS. RABBIT: [*to the others*] I know we are anxious, but we mustn't worry him. It takes time, you know. [*Suddenly there is a glow of light behind the rock and music is heard. Then out from behind the rock rises a large, beautifully coloured butterfly. The bird flies off stage left.*]

ALL THE ANIMALS TOGETHER: Oh-h-h!

MRS. RABBIT: Isn't it beautiful. Why, Clarence, you are the best of them all.

SAMMY: That was certainly worth waiting for.
[*Clarence has been flying around and is now joined by the other two butterflies, but he is bigger than either of them.*]

MR. SQUIRREL: Look, he is bigger, too.

MRS. RABBIT: Well, to be like that was certainly worth waiting for. Now he will be happy again.
[*Clarence flies higher. The animals call out and wave goodbye to him.*]

MRS. RABBIT: Goodbye, Clarence.

MR. SQUIRREL: You look beautiful.

SAMMY: I'll bet you are happy now.
[*Clarence flies out and the animals continue waving and calling as the curtain closes.*]

Spider's Eye View

a one act play for marionettes by Elizabeth Merten

Characters

A LARGE SPIDER
A DRAGONFLY
BELINDA   a butterfly
MERVYN   a moth

Scene   A large spider's web — stretched against a sky background. Somewhere in the forest.

Music   Lizst's "Première Valse Oubliée", or similar piano music.

Production notes

This play for marionettes is designed primarily for an audience of older children and adults.

Naturally, the size of the characters has to be considerably exaggerated. The SPIDER could well be eighteen inches or more across, with the legs outstretched.

The personalities of the characters are well defined in the dialogue, but careful attention should be given to the voices in order to get the most out of them. The MOTH, of course, is almost static, and has so little to say that his voice can easily be doubled by whoever voices the DRAGONFLY.

The setting for the play is simplicity itself — a spider's web stretched against a blue sky. One or two rocks and a cut-out ground row of low bushes or grasses, will serve to break up the severe line between the sky and the floor of the stage, and perhaps a fallen tree trunk could form the lower anchor for the web.

A stretched blue backdrop will form the sky. Do not use too light a blue, because the stage lighting will cause it to appear several shades lighter than it looks in daylight.

The web can be made of thick string or cord. It will be necessary for the web to be suspended several inches away from the backdrop to allow space for the manipulation of the Moth. It has also to be sufficiently high for the top to be out of view of the audience, in order that the Spider may disappear during the dialogue between the Butterfly and the Moth.

More control will be possible when the Spider climbs the web if the bottom of the web is anchored about twelve inches further downstage than the top. This will provide an incline for the Spider.

Care should be taken that the Spider's manipulator can stretch out far enough to manipulate the Spider when it is on the ground. A special string could be attached to the front of the Spider which, when pulled, will cause the Spider to tilt to an angle that will make it easier for it to appear to climb the web.

A tree branch, angled upwards from one wing, would help the illusion that, somewhere higher up, the web is attached to the branch.

The Butterfly, Moth and Dragonfly can be constructed according to the suggestions given for the butterflies in the Production Notes for *All Change for Spring*, on page 11.

Spider's Eye View

[*As the curtain opens, the moth (in position behind the web at stage left) flutters weakly.*]

MOTH: [*faintly*] Help! Help! Help!

[*The Spider drops in from above at centre stage and lands facing audience.*]

SPIDER: Dear me, how bright it is all of a sudden. Never catch anybody in this light — may as well take a sun-bath for a while.

MOTH: [*faintly*] Help! Help!

SPIDER: Be quiet up there! My, it's good to stretch one's legs and relax. [*He waves his legs about and begins to sing lazily.*] When a spider's not engaged in his employment, his employment, or maturing his felonious little plans, little plans . . . [*The dragonfly flies in from stage left.*] Ah, dragonfly! Lovely weather we're having.

DRAGONFLY: [*flying the other way*] Oh dear, it's you, is it!

SPIDER: Don't go, I'm just in the mood for a chat.

DRAGONFLY: [*turning back*] What about?

SPIDER: Won't you come into my parlour and . . .

DRAGONFLY: Really, spider, your technique's rather out of date, isn't it?

SPIDER: I don't know what you mean. I wouldn't dream of . . .

DRAGONFLY: Oh no, naturally! Don't you know that people don't have parlours nowadays?

SPIDER: Oh, I'm not like you. I don't care about fashions, here today and gone tomorrow.

DRAGONFLY: Really, spider, that's a very tactless expression to use in front of me.

SPIDER: You're too sensitive, my friend, and anyway you're quite mistaken about my intentions. My doctor said positively no dragonflies this summer, so you're quite safe. Come and have a look at my beautiful new web.

DRAGONFLY: I can see it very well from here, but I must admit it *is* rather fine . . . quite a modern design for an old fogey like you.

SPIDER: Glad you like it — I took a refresher course in weaving last winter.

DRAGONFLY: Really quite functional, isn't it?

SPIDER: Eh?

DRAGONFLY: That means it really does what it's designed to do.

SPIDER: [*laughing appreciatively*] I'll say it does.

DRAGONFLY: Oh, you make me shudder!

SPIDER: But I mean it — the food's been better than ever this year. I even had a *bee* for dinner last week, as big as THAT. (*Moving two legs out wide.*] They'd never believe it at the Spider's Club but it was a good two inches long. Quite a struggle, of course, but I landed him all right in the end. Been a good year for mosquitoes too . . . real good sport, mosquitoes . . . plenty of fight in 'em . . .

MOTH: [*faintly*] Help! Help!

DRAGONFLY: [*horrified*] Oh, there's somebody up there!

SPIDER: Pay no attention; it's only a silly moth who flew in this morning. I'm saving him for the weekend.

DRAGONFLY: [*flying up and near the moth*] Why, he's a beautiful creature with orange wings and big, black eyes, filled with tears. [*He flies down near the spider.*] You're an unfeeling brute and I won't be a party to such behaviour. Goodbye! [*Dragonfly exits fast to stage left.*]

SPIDER: [*laughing*] Nobody asked you to the party, my lad. Oh dear, what it is to be so squeamish. Well now, I feel a little peckish and there's a very good grasshopper's leg in the larder, so I'll go up and have a snack, I think. [*He is drawn up and out. As he disappears, a pretty butterfly flutters in from stage-right and circles about in the air.*]

BUTTERFLY: [*breathlessly*] I wonder if this is the place the dragonfly meant. I, was awfully kind of him to stop and give me directions. Oh yest there's a big spider's web . . . and there's poor Mervyn up in the corner. Oh, how terrible! [*She flies up and hovers near the moth.*] Mervyn! Mervyn! It's me, Belinda!

MOTH: [*pathetically*] Oh Belinda, I never thought I'd see you again.

BUTTERFLY: You poor, poor darling.

MOTH: I'm all tied to this horrible web and can't move hand or foot. Go away at once, or he'll trap you too.

BUTTERFLY: No, the dragonfly said he's not so cunning as he thinks he is, so I'm going to try something that might save you. I'm going away for a minute, Mervyn dear, but I'll be back, so be brave and keep your antennae crossed. [*She dances off-stage right and the spider drops down again.*]

SPIDER: Well, that was very tasty. Now all I need is a little light entertainment to pass the time and everything would be perfect. And here we are — just what the doctor ordered — how delightful. [*The butterfly flutters on again from stage-right, dancing in the air to the soft music of Liszt's "Première Valse Oubliée" or similar piano music. Near the end the spider comments:*] Isn't she charming? Reminds me of that little ballet-dancer I used to admire when I had my winter web at the Opera-house — so sweetly young and innocent. Careful, my dear, don't catch your wings in the web! Gracious, what am I saying? [*Butterfly comes to rest on a stone near the spider.*]

BUTTERFLY: [*with a silvery laugh*] Hello, Mr. Spider. I'm Belinda Butterfly . . . how did you like my dance?

SPIDER: It was enchanting, Miss Belinda, but don't you know this is no place for a young lady like you?

BUTTERFLY: Why ever not, Mr. Spider?

SPIDER: Because . . . well, because . . . Oh my ten-legged uncle, I wish she'd flutter off; my self-control is slipping!

20

BUTTERFLY: Whatever's wrong, Mr. Spider? Don't you care for butterflies?

SPIDER: Too much, my dear . . . too much.

BUTTERFLY: Then I really don't know what you are trying to say, but I think you're sweet anyway. I'm going to give you a kiss, just for enjoying my dance.

SPIDER: [*as she kisses him*] Oh my sixteen-legged aunt! [*He waves his legs wildly.*]

BUTTERFLY: There.

SPIDER: What an extremely rash young female you are! Aren't you afraid of me?

BUTTERFLY: Afraid of a dear old furry spider like you? No. Should I be?

SPIDER: Yes . . . no . . . oh, I don't know . . . you've got me all confused.

BUTTERFLY: Yes, you do look a bit tangled. I'm sorry if I'm upsetting you, but I'd like to ask you a very important question before I go.

SPIDER: Yes, yes, anything, but be quick about it.

BUTTERFLY: Have you seen a young moth passing this way . . . one with a perfectly beautiful expression?

SPIDER: [*embarrassed*] Well . . . ermph . . . I'm not in the habit of looking at the expressions of moths . . .

BUTTERFLY: Well, there's no need to be embarrassed about it, you sweet old thing!

SPIDER: [*very uncomfortably*] Isn't there?

BUTTERFLY: No, just say if you saw a moth or not . . .

SPIDER: Well, I did see one . . . about five minutes ago . . . but . . .

BUTTERFLY: With what colour of wings?

SPIDER: [*feebly*] Orange, I think.

BUTTERFLY: Then that's him. That's my Mervyn. Where is he now? [*She looks up towards the corner where the moth is and the spider moves to block her vision.*]

SPIDER: [*hastily*] He flew off that way. [*Pointing off-stage right.*] Why don't you hurry after him?

BUTTERFLY: [*hedging*] But I've been over there already and he wasn't there. Are you sure he isn't here?

SPIDER: Sure, sure? Of course I'm sure — now go on, what are you waiting for?

BUTTERFLY: Well, well, perhaps if I wait here, he'll come back?

SPIDER: Now, listen to me, young lady — if you don't go now, it'll be too late for both of you.

BUTTERFLY: Oh dear! Well, if you do happen to see Mervyn again . . .

SPIDER: I'll tell him you're looking for him.

BUTTERFLY: Promise?

SPIDER: Promise.

BUTTERFLY: Oh, thank you — what a good, kind spider you are! Goodbye. [*She flies off stage-right.*]

SPIDER: [*exhausted*] Whew! I thought she'd never go! M'm'm, looked so appetizing too. I wonder where she got those crazy ideas about spiders from? Dear? Kind? Good? And there was her friend with the beautiful expression up in the corner all the time . . . ha, ha, ha. [*He looks up and then climbs up in front of the moth.*] Hallo there, Mervyn. Did you see your girl-friend kissing me, Mervyn? She kissed a black-hearted, ugly old spider for the first time in his life! [*He should try to give the impression of untying the moth as he speaks.*] Seems to me she needs someone to look after her before she gets into serious trouble, so you'd better come out and shake your wings and be off, before I change my mind. [*The moth slips out from behind the web and re-enters fluttering in front of it. He flies straight across stage from left to right and out.*] Goodbye, Mervyn, you lucky fellow. [*Pause.*] Not a word of thanks. Can you beat that? Mind you, this is not a story I'd care to have other spiders know about, so just keep it to yourselves, will you?
[*Curtain.*]

The King of Puppetania

a one act play for hand puppets by George Merten

Characters

KING DIDDLE	
LORD FRAUD	the King's Chief Minister
HYSTERISIS	servant to Lord Fraud
TAX COLLECTOR	
THE PRINCESS	
MADAME CRONE	the Kingdom Witch
HER DAUGHTER	
SPINDLE	son of the chief screw-eye maker

Property Thinking Cap

Scene A room in the Palace of The King of Puppetania.

Production notes

This play is more suitable for presentation to adults and older children and is designed for hand puppets.

The play can be staged very simply in drapes. These should be sufficiently rich looking to suggest a chamber in the Royal Palace, but should not be so brilliant as to overwhelm the puppets.

The voice for each character should be chosen with particular care. Not only is this necessary to bring out the satirical qualities of the play, but there is at times a good deal of dialogue without a great amount of obvious action. Considerable subtlety is required from the acting at all times and there is an opportunity here to develop some interesting characteristics in the players. Small but significant movements will be particularly effective.

THE KING is obviously of the old school, starched stiff with protocol.

THE PRINCESS does not have a very large part, although it is one of the essentials of the play. In her four brief speeches as the ugly princess, she exhibits a certain eagerness and affectation that would be not only unseemly but quite unnecessary in a princess, and much more in the character of the daughter of a witch elevated beyond her station.

The princess's character changes completely during the closing stages of the play with the switching of the heads. She becomes what is usually accepted as the traditional type of fairy story princess.

LORD FRAUD is naturally a somewhat pompous and therefore ridiculous character, but he has had some of his pomposity shaken by the turn of events and the implied, threat to his position. He provides the lightest touch in the play.

THE TAX COLLECTOR is, generally speaking, a solid character and a supplier of information essential to the plot.

HYSTERISIS could develop into a light, bright character, usually very efficient, but without too much respect for his master's cerebral exercises.

MADAME CRONE is of the school of pure fantasy. A cunning subservience, despite her favourable bargaining position, is her chief characteristic.

SPINDLE, except for an appearance at the very end of the play, has no significant part. He is merely a pleasant-faced youth in peasant costume.

Obviously the heads of the Princess and Madame Crone's daughter cannot be secured to the necks of their respective bodies. Care should be taken, however, to ensure that this is not obvious to the audience. The infrequent appearances of these characters will make this illusion relatively simple to maintain. The exchanging of the heads is pure puppetry and couldn't be accomplished in any but a puppet theatre.

The only property is the Thinking Cap. This need not be difficult to construct. Since it should be very light in weight, papier mâché would be the best material. The helmet is dome-shaped, like a space helmet and is painted aluminum colour. It has a perspex panel set in the front, with three small lamps in behind the panel, one each red, green and amber. They are wired to a small switchboard that can be brought in by Hysterisis and placed on the playboard. Hysterisis operates the three push-button switches necessary to light up the lamps in the helmet. The helmet is quite large and tends to drop over Lord Fraud's ears, but is prevented from falling right down over his head by a wire mesh (fine chicken wire) which is placed across the inside of the helmet at the correct height and shaped to fit the top of Lord Fraud's head.

The small battery necessary to light the lamps can be stored in the helmet or on the switchboard. The latter arrangement would facilitate a quicker system of replacement and also prevent undesirable weight being added to the helmet.

The King of Puppetania

[*As the curtain opens Lord Fraud is seen on stage in an attitude of deep thought. A moment later the King enters from stage-left.*]

KING: Lord Fraud, we need more money.

LORD FRAUD: [*A little startled, not having heard the King enter.*] Yes, yes, Your Majesty, but how do we propose to get it?

KING: Be more precise, Fraud. How do YOU propose to get it?

LORD FRAUD: I have used up all the ways I know, sire. I have raised the taxes . . .

KING: Then raise them again.

LORD FRAUD: But, Your Majesty, the people cannot stand any more taxation, and still keep up their payments.

KING: Then they will have to fall behind on their payments . . .

LORD FRAUD: But Your Majesty . . .

KING: Can't you say anything but "But Your Majesty"?

LORD FRAUD: Well, yes, I can, but you may not like it.

KING: I don't like anything you've said so far.

LORD FRAUD: Your Majesty, if the puppets fall behind on their payments, then *we* lose because their payments come to our Royal Finance and Benevolent Loan Corporation. And besides, sire, if they can't continue to pay for their new model heads, hands, costumes and all the other things, we shall have many other problems as well.

KING: But we must have more money.

LORD FRAUD: I know, Your Majesty, but if the payments aren't kept up we shall have our stores full of goods, and so there will be unemployment besides. Not only that, sire, but there will be great discontent among the puppulace and many of them will be shabby and wearing the old look.

KING: No doubt something could be . . .

LORD FRAUD: [*interrupting*] Worse yet, sire. Not only will we have this year's models on our hands, but what about next year's new models? The thought makes my paint peel.

KING: Well, something has to be done. I have to get my daughter, the Princess, married off. Otherwise what will happen to my line? I can't understand why all the suitors who come along say that the dowry is not enough. Not only that, but each one wants more and more.

LORD FRAUD: [*embarrassed*] I . . . I suppose it depends on what each one expects, . . . er . . . I mean . . . er . . . not everyone is suited to everyone, Your Majesty.

KING: But my daughter MUST marry!

LORD FRAUD: [*hesitatingly*] Do you not think that perhaps a . . . a . . . er . . . new model . . .

KING: What do you mean, Fraud?

LORD FRAUD: Nothing, sire, only . . .

25

KING: You know I consider that the habit of new models of this and that every year is for the common puppulace, not for Royalty, Fraud. After all, whom do *I* need to impress?

LORD FRAUD: Nobody, of course, Your Majesty, nobody at all.

KING: I'm going back to my gold hook now and I suggest you put on your thinking cap, Fraud, and come up with a solution if you expect to continue to enjoy the privileges of your office. [*King exits stage left. Lord Fraud moves up and down, obviously thinking. He stops and calls off-stage right.*]

LORD FRAUD: Hysterisis! [*Hysterisis enters.*]

HYSTERISIS: Yes, m'lord, you called?

LORD FRAUD: Bring me my Thinking Cap, Hysterisis. I have a problem.

HYSTERISIS: Yes, m'lord. [*He turns to exit stage right.*]

LORD FRAUD: One moment! Send someone for the Collector of Taxes. I want to see him at once.

HYSTERISIS: Yes, m'lord. [*Exits stage right.*]

LORD FRAUD: [*to audience*] Problems, nothing but problems. It doesn't matter how much more money I raise, nobody will want to marry the Princess anyway. Have YOU seen her? Ugh! [*Enter the Collector of Taxes, stage left.*]

COLLECTOR: You sent for me, Lord Fraud?

LORD FRAUD: Yes, I did. How can we raise more money?

COLLECTOR: That is impossible, my lord. We have used every means that existed and some we invented. If we are not careful we might have deflation.

LORD FRAUD: I know, I know. Do you think we can have another Kingdom Bond issue.

COLLECTOR: No, my lord, much too soon.

LORD FRAUD: What a pity. Then how can we raise enough money?

COLLECTOR: I don't know, my lord. If only King Diddle would give up trying to get his daughter married!

LORD FRAUD: There seems to be no way of telling him that she has too many natural disadvantages, poor girl. Why, the year the King had her portrait put on the stamps, all the letters came back. The worst of it is, it doesn't really matter how much money he has for the dowry, he will never get anybody to accept her. They will always want more, if only as an excuse to get away. [*Hysterisis enters stage right with the Thinking Cap.*] Ah, here is my Thinking Cap. Perhaps I can get a new idea.

COLLECTOR: Well, my lord, I hope you can think up some way out of this situation. I am completely baffled.

LORD FRAUD: I will try. Come, Hysterisis, put my Thinking Cap on for me. [*Hysterisis places the helmet on Lord Fraud's head, with the panel to*

26

the front. He puts the switch panel in a comfortable position on the playboard and is ready to operate.]

HYSTERISIS: Are you ready, m'lord?

LORD FRAUD: Yes, yes, switch on. [*Hysterisis pushes the amber switch. The Collector is watching closely.*]

HYSTERISIS: The preliminary thought light is on, m'lord.

LORD FRAUD: Yes, I can feel something beginning to stir. Now I am ready for full thought. Give me full thought for easy answers, Hysterisis. [*Hysterisis presses the red button. The light in the panel changes to red. Lord Fraud begins to move in a slightly rhythmic manner. The Collector looks at him.*]

COLLECTOR: Are you having any thoughts, my lord?

LORD FRAUD: Yes, I am. They are very pleasant, but they have nothing to do with the problem. [*Turning to Hysterisis.*] Are you sure you have connected the right attachment for Easy Answers?

HYSTERISIS: Easy Answers, m'lord? I thought you said Eastern Dancers!

LORD FRAUD: Well, change it immediately. This is business hours, you know. [*Hysterisis presses the green switch and the panel shows green.*]

COLLECTOR: Have you an idea yet, my lord?

LORD FRAUD: Nothing new, only some of the old ones again. Wait a minute! There is something simmering now . . .[*pause*] . . . what about this? Can't we manufacture papier-mâché money? Then we can make all we need.

COLLECTOR: But, my lord, we do not have enough security to cover extra money. Besides, it would cause TOO much inflation. We don't want people to have more money than there are goods to buy.

LORD FRAUD: That would put prices up.

COLLECTOR: Yes, but don't forget that *we* have the goods and we know the money is not worth what it should be, so all we would get is the useless money back again.

LORD FRAUD: I suppose you are right. I had forgotten that. I will think once more. Hysterisis, give me plenty of power. [*Hysterisis presses all the buttons in rapid succession several times, causing a confusion of changing lights.*]

LORD FRAUD: Yes! No! That's it! No, it isn't. I think I have it. No, I don't. Oh dear, I am quite confused. [*Hysterisis now keeps the green light on.*]

LORD FRAUD: Ah, I am thinking more clearly now. Yes, I have another idea.

COLLECTOR: [*anxiously*]: What is it, my lord?

LORD FRAUD: Take this thing off, Hysterisis, I am quite exhausted. Take it away. [*Hysterisis removes the helmet from Lord Fraud's head and exits with the helmet and the switchboard to stage right.*]

LORD FRAUD: [*with helmet off*] That is better. Now I can think. Let me see, the idea I had was this. What we need are some natural resources. That should solve our problems.

COLLECTOR: Yes, indeed it would, my lord, but we cannot create natural resources. Unless we happen to discover them, it doesn't help us.

LORD FRAUD: No, I suppose you are right, but I did think of a solution, didn't I?

[*The King enters stage right, followed by the Princess, who is excessively ugly.*]

KING: Well, Lord Fraud, did you put your thinking cap on?

LORD FRAUD: Yes, Your Majesty.

KING: And what did it produce?

LORD FRAUD: I had some ideas, sire, but the Collector of Taxes said they wouldn't work.

KING: Then you had better have some that will. I have promised my daughter that by next week there will be enough dowry to satisfy any suitor. And, if there isn't . . . you are not yet married, are you, Lord Fraud? [*The Princess moves towards Lord Fraud, who hastily backs away.*]

LORD FRAUD: No, sire, not yet, but . . . but . . . I . . . I . . . have some plans . . .

KING: And so have I, Fraud. [*Turning to the Princess.*] Come, daughter. [*They begin to exit stage right.*] He isn't worthy of you, and he isn't the match I would like, but he wouldn't dare claim a dowry. [*King and Princess exit, leaving Lord Fraud and Collector on stage.*]

COLLECTOR: It looks, my lord, as though you will have to get a new Thinking Cap. Still, the King's idea would save the whole Kingdom from . . .

LORD FRAUD: No! No! No! There must be some other way. Why won't he listen to me and give her a new head? After all, I have had three myself.

COLLECTOR: But you are always recognisable, the character doesn't change.

LORD FRAUD: Any change in the Princess would be an improvement.

COLLECTOR: Do you require me further, my lord? If not, I have work to attend to. It is no easy matter collecting these extra taxes, even the hidden ones.

LORD FRAUD: No, you may go. I must keep thinking or the King will make me marry that ghastly . . . [*looking around in sudden fear of being overheard*] . . . I mean, the Princess, as if all this were my fault.

COLLECTOR: Thank you, my lord. [*Exits stage left.*]

LORD FRAUD: [*to audience*] How am I ever going to get out of this situation? If I do raise more money it won't help. If I don't raise more money, the King will make me marry the Princess. I wonder if I should leave Puppetania . . . [*Hysterisis has entered stage right.*]

HYSTERISIS: M'lord!

LORD FRAUD: [*displeased*] Yes, Hysterisis? What now?

HYSTERISIS: The Kingdom Witch, Madame Crone, is here to see you, m'lord.

LORD FRAUD: [*sharply*] What does she want?

HYSTERISIS: She wouldn't say, m'lord, only that it is important and to do with the Princess.

LORD FRAUD: To do with the Princess! Send her in. [*Hysterisis exits stage right.*]

LORD FRAUD: [*to audience*] I wonder what Madame Crone wants? She hasn't been much help to me since we taxed her spells. [*Madame Crone enters stage right.*]

LORD FRAUD: [*turning to Madame Crone*] Well, Madame Crone, you wished to see me?

MADAME CRONE: Yes, your lordship. Things are not good in Puppetania, your lordship, what with the taxes . . .

LORD FRAUD: [*interrupting with exasperation*] Do you think I don't know that? Is that all you came to tell me?

MADAME CRONE: Oh no, your lordship; that isn't all by any means. [*cackles*] I hear your lordship is going to marry the Princess perhaps? [*more cackles*]

LORD FRAUD: [*furious*] How did you know that? Who has been talking? Anyway, I'm not . . . at least . . . er . . .

MADAME CRONE: I hear many things, your lordship, and my crystal reveals the closest secrets.

LORD FRAUD: I'll put a tax on your crystal if you spread gossip about me, you wicked old crone.

MADAME CRONE: And would you take off all these taxes if you had the answer to getting the Princess married . . . to someone else, of course?

LORD FRAUD: If we could do that there wouldn't be any need for the taxes. Do you know how it can be done? If so, speak at once.

MADAME CRONE: Yes, I know how it can be done, but first I must make a bargain with the King.

LORD FRAUD: Are you mad, old woman? Nobody can bargain with the King.

MADAME CRONE: Perhaps you could, Lord Fraud. Especially if it saved you from marrying the Princess.

LORD FRAUD: Well, I'd try anything to stop that. It wouldn't be so bad if she was as beautiful as your own daughter, but I still . . .

MADAME CRONE: [*cunningly*] Perhaps she could be, your lordship?

LORD FRAUD: What's that? Could you make her grow beautiful? You know the King will not listen to anyone in the Royal Family having a new head. I have tried that.

MADAME CRONE: [*craftily*] Not a *new* head. That would be too easy. Just the right head, that is all.

LORD FRAUD: The right head! What do you mean, witch? Tell me at once.

MADAME CRONE: I have to make a bargain, your lordship. *You* must get the King to agree to my bargain.

LORD FRAUD: [*angrily*] Tell me the answer, crone, or I will have you locked up.

MADAME CRONE: And while I am locked up, your lordship will marry the Princess.

LORD FRAUD: Don't talk about that! All right, what is this bargain you want to make?

MADAME CRONE: I cannot tell you what the bargain is. You must get the King to promise to listen to me and agree to my bargain when I do make it.

LORD FRAUD: [*aghast*] You won't tell *me* what it is. Then how do you expect me to get the King to agree? It is impossible!

MADAME CRONE: I think he will make any bargain to get his daughter suitably married, your lordship.

LORD FRAUD: Yes, perhaps he will. What do you mean by *suitably* married, crone?

MADAME CRONE: Nothing, your lordship, except that the Princess will have a suitor before the day is out, without such a big dowry. Will your lordship see the King?

LORD FRAUD: [*reluctantly*] I'll see him, but I doubt if he will agree to a bargain he knows nothing about. Listen! I hear him coming! [*He listens.*] Yes, quickly now, you must go, but not too far away in case I need you — quietly now — [*Lord Fraud ushers Madame Crone off stage right. King enters stage left.*]

KING: Well, Fraud, have you had any more ideas?

LORD FRAUD: Yes, Your Majesty, I mean No, Your Majesty —

KING: Yes, no. What do you mean, Fraud? Have you or haven't you?

LORD FRAUD: [*embarrassed*] It is a little difficult to say, sire. It isn't an idea, exactly, it's . . . it's . . .

KING: [*impatiently*] It's what, Fraud?

LORD FRAUD: [*hesitatingly*] Sire, it seems that Madame Crone — that is, the Kingdom Witch —

KING: Yes, yes, I know.

LORD FRAUD: Well, sire, it seems that she thinks she can put all this right —

KING: [*still impatiently*] Put all what right?

LORD FRAUD: [*very uncomfortable*] It seems, sire, that she has the answer —

KING: [*in exasperation*] What do you mean by "it seems, it seems"? Do you have anything to tell me, or don't you? And what has the witch got to do with it?

LORD FRAUD: [*very unhappily*] If Your Majesty will show tolerance for a moment I will try and explain this curious situation.

KING: [*threateningly*] I hope you can, Fraud — go on.

LORD FRAUD: The witch came to me, sire, and said that she can make it certain that the very next suitor will marry the Princess and without requesting a large dowry and —

KING: You send for her at once —

LORD FRAUD: There was a condition, Your Majesty —

KING: [*angrily*] CONDITION! Who talks to me of conditions? I will not listen to conditions. [*He reflects for a moment.*] What is the condition, Fraud?

LORD FRAUD: I do not know, sire. She only wants me to ask your promise that you will grant her condition —

KING: [loudly] Accept the conditions of one of my own subjects! That is ridiculous. Especially when I don't even know what it is. [Princess enters stage left.]

PRINCESS: What is it, Father? You sound angry.

KING: The witch is trying to make me accept a condition I don't even know before she will tell me what she knows about suitors — your marriage and — oh, I don't know what to make of it.

PRINCESS: [eagerly] Is there another suitor, Father?

KING: No, there isn't! But the witch says the next one will marry you if I grant her condition.

PRINCESS: [deliberately] Of course, I should have to consider his proposal first.

KING: What's that? Oh yes, of course, my dear ... er ... but not too long.

PRINCESS: Then you may as well agree to the condition, Father.

KING: Don't you understand, daughter, it is the principle of the thing.

LORD FRAUD: If I may be permitted to say so, Your Majesty, I see no other alternative.

KING: You are not permitted to say so, Fraud. I will think this out for myself. [pause] I don't like it, but I can't see any alternative.

LORD FRAUD: Is that your decision, sire?

KING: It is the only one I can make. Send the old witch here, Fraud.

LORD FRAUD: She is outside awaiting your pleasure, sire. I will have her brought in at once. [Lord Fraud moves to stage right and calls.] Hysterisis! [Hysterisis enters stage right.]

HYSTERISIS: You called, m'lord?

LORD FRAUD: Tell Madame Crone she is summoned to the King's presence.

HYSTERISIS: Yes, m'lord. [Hysterisis exits stage right.]

KING: I don't like this, Fraud. I don't like this at all.

LORD FRAUD: [who is looking off stage right] No, Your Majesty, but here is Madame Crone, and she has her daughter with her. [Madame Crone enters stage right followed by a beautiful girl, who is also dressed in the garb of a witch.]

MADAME CRONE: [ingratiatingly] Your Majesty is kind indeed to listen to a poor old witch. Lord Fraud has acquainted you with my most humble request, Your Majesty?

KING: He has acquainted me with your most impertinent demands, crone. This girl, I take it, is your daughter?

MADAME CRONE: Yes, Your Majesty.

KING: Well, waste no more time. I will accept your condition, provided that whatever you prophesy comes to pass. Now, what is your condition?

MADAME CRONE: Very simple, Your Majesty. It is that after I have told you my story, you will spare my life and allow me to continue to be the Kingdom Witch.

31

KING: All right, I agree, but tell your story quickly.

MADAME CRONE: Your Majesty is too kind. My tale will not take long to tell. You will notice that my daughter is very beautiful, much too beautiful to be a successful witch? Everyone wants to marry her.

KING: Everyone wants to marry her? Yes, yes, I can understand that. But go on, woman.

MADAME CRONE: You will notice, Your Majesty, that the Princess and my daughter are about the same age. When they were but a few weeks old I flew in through the Palace windows one night and exchanged the heads of the Princess and my daughter.

KING: [*enraged*] You did that, you wicked old crone? I'll have you burned —

MADAME CRONE: I have your Royal promise, Your Majesty; you would not break that. [*The King is very agitated and at a loss for adequate speech. He is indulging in a kind of Royal splutter.*] I know I shouldn't have done it, Your Majesty, but I could see that my daughter was going to look like me, and I did so want her to be beautiful. But she is far too beautiful for the business of being a witch. She spends so long admiring herself and considering all her offers of marriage that she has no time to learn her spells and potions. Besides that, the whole Kingdom is unhappy because of all the extra taxes, so I decided to throw myself upon Your Majesty's most gracious clemency.

KING: [*somewhat recovered*] You took good care that I had to show clemency first, witch!

MADAME CRONE: Merely an elementary precaution, Your Majesty. I am now ready to put things right — by changing the heads back again.

KING: I have said my daughter must not have a new head —

LORD FRAUD: But, sire, it will not be a new head, but her own head.

KING: Yes, of course, I had forgotten that. Well, witch, give me my real daughter back at once.

MADAME CRONE: There is little harm done really, Your Majesty. She is still a very sweet girl and never did learn my spells — she didn't have the head for it. [*cackles*] Now, perhaps Lord Fraud would kindly assist me?

LORD FRAUD: I'll do anything to put this right. What shall I do, Madame Crone? [*During her own and Lord Fraud's speech Madame Crone has taken the Princess's head off and now hands it to Lord Fraud to hold.*]

LORD FRAUD: [*aside to audience*] That improves her already. [*Madame Crone now removes her daughter's head and places it on the Princess, while the King watches anxiously.*]

KING: That certainly does make a difference. It is a funny thing I didn't notice what was wrong before. Well, daughter, and how do you feel? [*Madame Crone has taken the head from Lord Fraud and put it on her own daughter.*]

PRINCESS: [*in a pleasant voice*] It seems strange to wear these beautiful clothes, but I am sure I shall soon get used to it. I wonder how Spindle will like me now?

KING: Spindle? Who's that?

PRINCESS: He is the son of the chief screw-eye maker. This morning he asked me to marry him and I promised.

KING: Screw-eye maker! My daughter married to the son of a screw-eye maker! Ridiculous!

LORD FRAUD: There wouldn't be any dowry to worry about, Your Majesty.

KING: But we have it now.

LORD FRAUD: It could be used as surplus to reduce the taxes and the puppulace would be happy again, sire. But if you don't like [*turning to Princess*] Spindle (was it not, Princess?), then you did suggest that I —

KING: You were just a makeshift, Fraud. This is quite a problem [*turning to the Princess*] — you are sure you promised to marry this — this Spindle as you call him? [*Hysterisis rushes in stage right.*]

HYSTERISIS: M'lord, m'lord!

LORD FRAUD: What do you mean by coming into the King's presence like this, Hysterisis?

HYSTERISIS: The Mayor, on behalf of all the puppets, insisted that you be told the news immediately, m'lord.

KING: What news is this? What more news can there be?

HYSTERISIS: One of the puppets was prospecting today and has discovered a large plastic wood deposit, Your Majesty.

KING and LORD FRAUD together: PLASTIC WOOD DEPOSIT!

KING: Who found it?

HYSTERISIS: Spindle, Your Majesty, the son of the screw-eye maker.

LORD FRAUD: Natural resources mean great wealth, sire, and the end of all our troubles.

KING: Is this the Spindle that my daughter wishes to marry, Lord Fraud?

LORD FRAUD: It must be, Your Majesty, there is only one chief screw-eye maker in the Kingdom.

KING: Then, as a rich and famous puppet, he would make an ideal match for the Princess. Summon him here. [*Hysterisis exits stage right.*]

KING: [*turning to the others*] This is indeed a surprising day. And as for you, Madame Crone, I feel I should be angry with you, but things seem to be turning out very well after all, so I'll forget it. [*Spindle enters stage left and moves towards the Princess, who turns towards him.*]

KING: [*to Spindle*] So you are Spindle. Well, as always happens in those idiotic fairy stories, all ends happily and you may marry the Princess. Make the arrangements, Fraud. [*Waves arms in dismissal.*] Everybody go away now while I recover from all this. [*Puppets bow to King and move towards exits as curtains close.*]

Wiggie In The Jungle

a one-act play for sock-puppets, designed for a very young audience
by Elizabeth Merten

Characters

WIGGIE PIGLET
MRS. OSTRICH
HERBIE HIPPO
EDWARD ELEPHANT

Properties   a worm
spectacles for Herbie Hippo

Scene   A clearing in the jungle

Production notes

There is no difficult manipulation to this play, which can easily be performed by young children.

It is described as being for sock puppets, but could be presented just as easily with hand puppets.

The jungle clearing scene for the play can be made very simply by sewing cut-out materials, to represent trees and foliage, on to a background of scrim (theatrical gauze), or other suitable open weave material. Since the manipulators have to see through the backdrop, without themselves being seen by the audience (assuming that the operation is not overhead), care should be exercised so to arrange the decor that it does not entirely block the manipulator's view of the puppets. It is also effective to arrange some foliage, or rocks, at each end of the playboard. Any scenery or properties used in this way should be kept as close to the proscenium as possible in order not to take up too much of the acting area and also not to block the view of that part of the audience seated on the sides.

The play can be given by two manipulators, each using two puppets, but a different manipulator can be used for each puppet if so desired. The stage lighting in any hand puppet stage when a "scrim" background is used should be directed to "cross" the background, not shine directly "through" it, otherwise the outlines of the manipulators may be visible to the audience. Try different light arrangements until the most satisfactory position is found.

The characters are basically sock puppets, but they can be built up more nearly to the relative proportions of their species by using the principles of stuffed toy construction, that is, by cutting out the profiles in felt or velvet and filling in the width of the head with a centre panel. All the seams are sewn. The space between the sock and the outside shape is stuffed with any convenient material.

Using the sock puppet as a base gives a considerable animation to the face and also a mouth movement.

Children can easily design and sew sock puppets and, if they wish to build and present the play quickly, they will achieve a very satisfactory result without elaborating the figures beyond the stage of simple sock puppets.

Wiggie In The Jungle

[*Wiggie Piglet enters from stage left, as curtains open, looking all around.*]

WIGGIE: I never thought the jungle would be like this! The branches are so thick you can hardly see the sky; and that big, dark river's not a bit like the shining one that runs beside our farm at home. But I'm very thirsty so I'd better have a drink. [*He bends over with back to audience.*] Schloop! Schloop! Schloop! [*Mrs. Ostrich looks in from stage right, observes Wiggie's back view and pecks him.*]

WIGGIE: [*squeaking*] Ee-ee-ee-ee-eeh! [*He straightens up, facing Mrs. O.*]

MRS. O.: Oh, my goodness! I beg your pardon! I thought you were a new kind of mushroom.

WIGGIE: Well, I'm Wiggie Piglet, and you nearly made me choke.

MRS. O.: I'm very sorry, Wiggie. My name is Mrs. Ostrich, and I've never seen anyone as round and pink as you before. Where do you live?

WIGGIE: At the white farm outside the jungle and now I know why my mother told me never to come in here. People peck you behind your back!

MRS. O.: Oh no, that was just a little mistake.

WIGGIE: A *little* mistake!

MRS. O.: But you really are too young to be wandering about alone. Why don't you run along home, like a good child?

WIGGIE: Do you know the farm where I live?

MRS. O.: No, I'm far too busy with my chicks to see much of the outside world, I'm afraid.

WIGGIE: Well, is there anybody who *might* know the way there?

MRS. O.: Wiggie Piglet, you're not lost, are you?

WIGGIE: [*hanging his head*] Well, I am, rather.

MRS. O.: Oh dear! Well, never mind, come along with me and have lunch with my children and we'll think of something.

WIGGIE: No, thank you, Mrs. Ostrich; they might think I *was* the lunch. I'd rather stay here.

MRS. O.: All right, then, you stay here until Edward Elephant comes by on his morning walk. He always knows the way to anywhere and you ask him.

WIGGIE: Edward Elephant? Who's he?

MRS. O.: He's a huge, grey animal, about twenty times as big as you.

WIGGIE: Ooh!

MRS. O.: He has a marvellous memory and he's a very helpful person.

WIGGIE: Oh good!

MRS. O.: So you have a little rest and wait here for Edward, and you'll be all right. I must hurry along home and feed my chicks now. [*Mrs. Ostrich exits to stage right.*]

WIGGIE: Bye bye. [*He sighs.*] Oh well. [*He lies down to rest at stage left.*]

[*Herbie Hippo's nose appears, moving along behind playboard from stage left, turning and moving to and fro several times. Wiggie gets up and gazes at the moving object.*]

WIGGIE: What can it be? It looks like a moving rock but how can it be that? [*Herbie lifts up his whole head above playboard.*] Ee-ee-ee-eeh! [*Wiggie runs off-stage left, squeaking.*]

HERBIE: Is there anybody here? [*He pauses and looks from side to side. Wiggie's head peeps out from left curtain but he is silent.*] That's funny — I thought I heard a kind of squeaking sound. Hello there! [*Pause*] Will someone please come and help me to find my glasses? [*Pause*] Oh well, I'll have another look under the water myself. [*He dives down below out of sight.*]

WIGGIE: [*re-entering cautiously from stage left*] I wonder if *he* could be Edward Elephant? He's very big and he's the right colour. He doesn't look very helpful and he seems to be a forgetful sort of person — but you never know. Maybe I'd better talk to him.

HERBIE: [*emerging at stage centre right*] No, I can't find them; what a nuisance. It's so embarrassing not to recognise people.

WIGGIE: Excuse me, sir.

HERBIE: Eh, who's that? Who are you? Come closer where I can see you. [*He looks the wrong way.*]

WIGGIE: I'm here, sir. [*Herbie swings round.*]

HERBIE: What? Ah, there you are. Why, you look like a round, pink . . .

WIGGIE: Mushroom, sir?

HERBIE: [*laughing heartily*] Ha, ha, ha . . . very funny. The idea of a talking mushroom . . . well, well. No, I was going to say a round, pink blob.

WIGGIE: Thank you very much. I'd rather be a mushroom than a blob. Are you Edward Elephant?

HERBIE: Am I Edward . . . did you say, am I Edward Elephant?

WIGGIE: Yes. What are you gasping for?

HERBIE: I'm absolutely speechless. I, Herbie Hippo, being mistaken for an elephant!

WIGGIE: After all, you mistook me for a blob.

HERBIE: That's an entirely different matter. I'm allowed to make mistakes because I'm short-sighted — you're not short-sighted, are you?

WIGGIE: No, my mother says I have very sharp eyes.

HERBIE: Then you have no excuse, no excuse at all. I'm very cross indeed.

WIGGIE: Well, Mrs. Ostrich said he's grey and twenty times bigger than me and that's what you are.

HERBIE: Oh, so Mrs. Ostrich is mixed up in this, is she? I might have known it. She's always taking a dig at me.

WIGGIE: She dug at me too, but she said it was not intended.

HERBIE: She's an interfering busybody, that's what she is.

MRS. O.: [*voice off*] Wiggie Piglet! Wiggie Piglet!

WIGGIE: It's her. [*Louder.*] I'm here, Mrs. Ostrich. [*Mrs. Ostrich puts her head in from stage right, with a very large worm in her beak. She can't see Wiggie behind Herbie's big head.*]

MRS. O.: [*speaking with her mouth closed*] Hello, Herbie, where's Wiggie?

HERBIE: What did you say?

WIGGIE: [*peeping round Herbie*] Here I am.

MRS. O.: [*mouth closed*] I brought you a nice, juicy worm for your lunch.

WIGGIE: [*squeaking, backing off*] Ee-ee-ee-eeh! I don't eat worms. Take it away, take it away.

HERBIE: Take it away from me too.

MRS. O.: [*mouth closed*] Nonsense, Wiggie. Come over here at once and open your mouth wide.

WIGGIE: I won't. [*He hides behind Herbie.*]

MRS. O.: Out of the way, Herbie. Children don't know what's good for them.

HERBIE: Now half a minute, Mrs. O. — we're not birds, you know.

MRS. O.: What? Oh, hoh, hoh — the thought of you flying through the air is too much for me, Herbie. [*She drops the worm during her laughter.*] Oh, hoh, hoh, hoh. I haven't had such a good laugh in months.

HERBIE: Now look here, Mrs. O. I've had enough of your jokes about me.

WIGGIE: [*whispering urgently*] It's all right now — she's dropped the worm in the river.

HERBIE: No, it's not all right. Why did you tell this piglet, if that's what he is . . .

WIGGIE: [*confidentially*] Yes, Wiggie Piglet.

HERBIE: This — this Wiggie that I was Edward Elephant?

MRS. O.: I did no such thing.

WIGGIE: No, no, she didn't, Herbie . . .

HERBIE: Well, why didn't you tell him I have a beautiful, broad nose — not a long, skinny trunk — I have neat, pointed ears — not great, loose ones that flap in the breeze — I have regular teeth, four of them — not long, bony tusks that stick out in front. If you'd only taken the trouble to tell Wiggie these things, he would have known me as soon as he saw me.

MRS. O.: He wasn't looking for you, Herbie — he was looking for Edward Elephant. And if you think I've got time to listen to a vain hippo talking about himself and to carry a heavy worm half-way through the jungle for a fussy piglet who won't eat it, you've made a big mistake. Goodbye. [*She exits to stage right.*]

WIGGIE: Oh dear, now *she's* insulted. I do seem to be causing a lot of trouble.

HERBIE: Just tell me one thing, Wiggie — was it true? Were you looking for Edward, not for me?

WIGGIE: [*gently*] Yes, Herbie . . . but I do think you're a beautiful hippo and I'm sorry I upset you. Is there anything I can do to show how sorry I am?

HERBIE: Well, there is one little thing, if you don't mind.

WIGGIE: You only have to say what it is.

HERBIE: You said you had sharp eyes, so please dive down in the river and find my glasses for me, there's a good fellow.

WIGGIE: Herbie! I can't swim. Think of something else.

HERBIE: But you don't need to swim — just hold your breath while you're down below and open your eyes and look around on the bottom.

WIGGIE: I'm terribly sorry but I've never been out of my depth, and I couldn't possibly. I would just drown, that's all.

HERBIE: Nonsense, I would keep an eye on you.

WIGGIE: What good would that do, I'd like to know.

HERBIE: Look, you'll enjoy it when you get in the water. Let me give you a little push with my nose . . . like this . . .

WIGGIE: [*squeaking and backing off*] No, no, no, no, no!

HERBIE: Yes, yes, YES. If you're going to be so difficult, Wiggie, I'll have to pick you up in my mouth and drop you in. [*Herbie takes Wiggie in his mouth. He struggles and squeaks and escapes, running off to stage left.*]

WIGGIE: Ee-ee-ee-ee-eeh! Help! Help!

HERBIE: I won't hurt you, you silly. [*He lunges about with his mouth open.*]
[*Edward Elephant enters from stage right.*]

EDWARD: Hello, Herbie, what's all the noise about?

HERBIE: Oh . . . er . . . is that you, Edward?

EDWARD: Yes. I thought I heard someone calling for help.

HERBIE: Oh . . . er . . . no, I didn't hear anything.

EDWARD: Really? I just met Mrs. Ostrich and she told me there was a lost piglet waiting here for me. Did you see him at all?

HERBIE: Well . . . er . . .

EDWARD: Now, Herbie, did you or didn't you?

HERBIE: Well, yes, there was one here but he's gone now. Excuse me, I have to find my glasses . . . [*He starts to dive.*]

EDWARD: Herbie, come back here. I haven't finished.

HERBIE: Oh, all right.

EDWARD: Now, what are you so embarrassed about?

HERBIE: Me? Embarrassed?

EDWARD: Herbie, did you scare that piglet away? [*No answer.*] Herbie, did you scare . . .

HERBIE: [*interrupting*] Yes, but I didn't mean it. I was trying to coax him to go into the water, that's all.

EDWARD: [*reproachfully*] Oh, Herbie. Which way did he go?

HERBIE: I couldn't see. He's very small, you know, like a little . . . [*sniff*] pink . . . [*sniff*] . . . blob . . . boo, hoo, hoo. I didn't mean it, Edward.

EDWARD: Don't upset yourself; we'll find him all right. I'll try this way first. [*Edward exits stage right; Herbie descends, sniffing and sighing, to below playboard. Wiggie returns from stage left.*]

WIGGIE: Oh dear, I'm back at the same place again. I must have run round in a circle. I hope that horrid Herbie won't come back, because I must have a little rest before I go on. [*Edward re-enters from stage right.*]

EDWARD: Ah, there you are at last. I'm Edward Elephant and Mrs. Ostrich has told me all about you.

WIGGIE: Oh, did she? That was very kind of her — I thought she didn't like me any more.

EDWARD: Oh, she has a good heart, though she gets a bit crotchety sometimes. Those chicks of hers keep her hopping, you know, but all the jungle people are kind to young things, as long as they don't try to hurt us.

WIGGIE: I know one who is very unkind to young things for no reason at all.

EDWARD: Ah, you mean Herbie? [*Wiggie nods.*] Well, he's really a very softhearted fellow too — it's just that sometimes he forgets how big and strong he is and he scares people. Do you know he cried after you ran away?

WIGGIE: Herbie cried?

EDWARD: Yes, and I think it would be very nice if you made friends with him again before I take you home.

WIGGIE: Oh, will you take me home?

EDWARD: Of course I will but first let's call Herbie up to say goodbye.

WIGGIE: I'll do it. Herbie, Herbie! I'm back. [*Herbie emerges between them wearing his glasses.*] Hello, Herbie, I'm sorry I ran away from you.

HERBIE: And I'm sorry I scared you, Wiggie. My, now I can see you, what a charming little creature you are.

WIGGIE: Thank you, Herbie. [*They rub each other's noses.*]

EDWARD: Good. Now, Wiggie, exactly where is that farm of yours?

WIGGIE: Outside the jungle, on the edge of a beautiful shining river.

EDWARD: Does it have a brown roof, and a green fence round it?

WIGGIE: That's it . . . that's it.

EDWARD: Then nothing could be easier, Wiggie, because you live by the same river as this, and all we have to do is to follow its course.

WIGGIE: Are you sure? My river is all sparkly and clear — this one's so dark.

EDWARD: That's only because the branches keep the sun out. That's why Herbie lives here, isn't it, Herbie? Because it's cool and shady?

HERBIE: Eh? Oh yes, that's right, I was thinking about something else.

WIGGIE: What were you thinking about, Herbie?

HERBIE: I was thinking that if you sat on my back, I could take you all the way down the river to your home.

EDWARD: What a good idea — it would be much quicker and much better than walking, wouldn't it?

WIGGIE: Oh yes . . . imagine me going home on a hippo's back!

HERBIE: Climb on then, and hold on tight.

WIGGIE: [*climbing on from Herbie's left side*] Oh, this is fun. Bye bye, Edward, and thank you for everything. I won't forget my jungle-friends.

EDWARD: Bye bye, little pink blob. [*Wiggie, on Herbie's back, glides off slowly to stage left, while Edward waves his trunk after him. Suggested musical background of "Auld Lang Syne" might swell up here as curtains close.*]

Captain Blackpatch

a play for marionettes in three scenes by George Merten

Characters

FISHERMAN'S WIFE
TIMOTHY — her son
CAPT. BLACKPATCH — the ghost of the old pirate
SHORTY JOHN GOLD — the ghost of the Captain's lieutenant
OTTO THE OCTOPUS — the Captain's pet
SIMON — Timothy's father
SWORDFISH

Various fish and other deep sea creatures

Properties Scene I. Rough table, rocking chair, straight chair, stool, pieces of tissue paper, sewing material, a small lamp, a small bottle, the father's note, some rope, netting and other oddments.

Scene II. Two or three rocks.

Scene III. Rocks, plant life and weeds, knife, fisherman's boat, chest of gold, scrim.

Scene I The interior of a poor fisherman's hut on the edge of the sea.

Scene II The beach near the hut.

Scene III Under the sea.

Production notes

THE FISHERMAN's WIFE should present no difficulty as a character. Since she is mourning her husband, she should be soberly dressed, but not necessarily in black. Although sad, she should have a pleasant face and not be in any way ugly or shrewish. It is only through recent misfortune that she is unhappy.

TIMOTHY is a lad in his early teens. He should be poorly dressed, but some colour in his costume would heighten the effect both in the hut and on the beach. His hands should be modelled so that the bottle and the note can be quickly and securely placed in them.

CAPTAIN BLACKPATCH should be a colourful character in his costuming, with high sea boots and a sword hanging at his side. The tops of the boots can be of soft, black leather, partly rolled down. He should wear a triangular hat for preference, to show his status, particularly if he does not wear a coat. The black patch is an important feature, since it has given him his name. The face should be painted to give a ghostly effect; but let his one eye shine brightly.

SHORTY JOHN GOLD is, as his name implies, short of stature, but otherwise a typical conception of a traditional pirate. He should not wear a hat, only a kerchief; his face should also appear ghostly.

OTTO should not be dead black, but a dark grey, and have large, white eyes with either black or strong green centres. Most of his construction, including the tentacles, can be carried out with foam rubber, covered with a soft material that will not impede the easy, flowing movement that the rubber should give. Soft springs, such as those found in window-shade rollers, can also be used for the tentacles, if preferred.

A circular control will be found most convenient for Otto. A large circle of wood with a central column, like the extended hub of a wheel, and a second wide rim, that sits on top of the other one and is free to move up and down, forms the main part of the control. Four body strings are attached to the main lower circle of wood, while at least two strings from different points on each tentacle pass through holes drilled in the lower section of the control and are then attached to the upper movable rim. By holding the central control in one hand and manipulating the free rim with the other, a great deal of effective movement can be obtained. Independent movement of some of the tentacles can be had by tilting the upper circle of the control.

SIMON should be a weather-beaten character dressed in typical deep sea fisherman's garb. Make sure that he is at least half a head taller than Timothy. His right hand should be formed to hold the knife for his fight with the swordfish.

THE SWORDFISH should be very large, even in comparison to the men. He should be quite fearsome. A simple construction would be to model his shape in plasticine and then over-cast in papier-mâché.* He can be strung on two strings from a single bar control, provided the strings are attached at least twelve inches apart. Since the Swordfish's movements are rapid it is unnecessary to have any moving parts, such as the fins or tail.

The various other fish can be made in the same way as the Swordfish. The same basic plasticine shape can be covered again and again according to how many fish of that size are required. The fish that raise the boat to the surface at the close of the play can be a shoal that has been used throughout the final scene.

43

Scene I. The table, chairs and stool are easily constructed. Care should be taken that the woman can fit easily into the rocking-chair. The tissue-paper is merely for effect and an electric fan can be used to blow it off the table, when the door is opened as Timothy enters and leaves the hut. If it is more convenient, the piece of sewing can be fastened permanently in the woman's hand.

For the lamp on the table, it is possible to buy a small lamp, in the shape of a lantern, which uses a flashlight battery.

A string can be attached to the top corner of each window shutter. Manipulation of the strings will close the shutters.

The bottle can easily be attached to Timothy's hand by using a cork with a shallow but wide head. The neck of the bottle is inserted in the boy's hand and the cork is then pushed in. The top of the cork will not allow the bottle to drop from the boy's hand. It will only take a few seconds to place the bottle in position.

The note can easily be attached to the other hand.

Scene II. The rocks can be made by forming shapes with chicken wire, which is nailed to a base board, and then covering the wire with layers of paper, which are pasted on. Paint when dry.

Scene III. Use the same rocks, in different positions, as were used for Scene II. The clumps of weeds can be made from strips of green coloured cloth, nailed to pieces of board painted the same colour as the sea-floor. The cloth strips can be held up by thin pieces of thread attached to another board, which can be clamped above the proscenium. Whenever possible, slight movement given to the weeds will heighten the general effect.

The knife can be made of wood and should jam tightly into the fisherman's hand. Covering the handle with cork will ensure a better grip.

The fisherman's boat can be a cut-out shape bent around the edge of a piece of wood of a long, oval shape. The wood must be wide enough for Simon and Timothy to stand on. The weight of the boat must be taken by two strings attached to each end of the wood and carried up to an H-shaped control, the same length as the boat. This will give stability to the boat when the "crew" is aboard. The fish can be lightly attached to the boat to give the appearance of lifting it.

Only the top of the chest will be seen, so this can also be of flat construction. For convenience, it could be cut out as part of the boat shape.

NOTE: It is suggested that suitable music be played during the scene-changes, which should be effected very rapidly. The music should maintain the mood of the play and also prepare the audience for the next scene.

Captain Blackpatch

Scene I [*The interior of the fisherman's hut shows a rough plank construction. There is a window in the back wall at centre stage left. Shutters are hinged on each side of the window on the inside. Some rope and netting and other oddments are lying around. The table is centre stage and the woman is seated in the rocking chair, sewing, at stage left of the table. The straight chair is at stage right of the table and the stool is in the corner upstage left. A lighted lamp and a few pieces of paper are on the table. Just before the curtain opens the sound of the wind and soft thunder is heard. The wind gets stronger as the curtain opens and there is a peal of thunder. After a few moments a young boy, roughly dressed, enters from stage right. This is Timothy. The woman looks up as the boy crosses to the table.*]

WOMAN: It is getting late, son. I was beginning to worry. How much did you get for your fish?

TIMOTHY: Only a few pennies, mother. They were so small it is a wonder anyone bought them at all. If I only had a boat I could go out to sea and catch some really big fish like the ones father used to catch.

WOMAN: I do not want you to go out in a boat fishing. It was just such a storm as this that took your poor father away from us. The same thing could happen to you . . .

TIMOTHY: But, mother . . . [*He sits in chair stage right of table.*]

WOMAN: No, Timothy. I know you want to be a fisherman like your father, but I wish you would learn some other trade, a trade that would keep you safe from such dangers as sudden storms at sea. [*The storm is increasing in intensity.*]

TIMOTHY: But even storms are not too dangerous if you have a good strong boat. That is what I can't understand. Father had the best and strongest boat on the coast and yet all the others weathered the same storm and he didn't. His boat wasn't even washed ashore; it just disappeared.

WOMAN: The currents could have taken it many leagues away and it could have been smashed to pieces on the rocks. Whatever happened to it, it is gone, and your poor father has gone too. You must find another trade, my son.

TIMOTHY: But we have always been fishermen, mother . . .

WOMAN: Please, Timothy, listen to what I say to you and do not bring me any more unhappiness.

TIMOTHY: I will try, mother. [*Timothy rises from the chair, crosses to the window and stares out at the storm, which is now abating. His mother sits rocking slowly in her chair. Timothy turns back from the window.*] I think I will go out to the beach for a while.

WOMAN: Must you go out in the storm, son?

TIMOTHY: It won't last much longer. It is only the wind that you hear now. [*He crosses to exit at stage right.*] I won't be long, [*As he exits a gust of wind blows the thin sheets of paper off the table. The woman stands up and makes a move as if to pick them up, but changes her mind and crosses to the window. She closes each shutter in turn.*]

WOMAN: Just like his father. Doesn't ever think of the danger. How I hate these storms! [*She finishes closing the shutters and returns to the chair. She has only been seated a few moments when there is another gust of wind and Timothy returns in a state of excitement. He has a bottle in one hand and a piece of paper in the other.*]

TIMOTHY: Look, mother! Look what I found at the water's edge, right opposite our house!

WOMAN: What is it, son? [*She gets to her feet and moves behind the table to where Timothy is standing.*]

TIMOTHY: It's a note to you from father; it was in this bottle.

WOMAN: Are you sure, Timothy?

TIMOTHY: Yes, so perhaps he is not dead! Listen to what the note says: [*He reads aloud.*] "My wife, something strange is happening in this storm. It is not like any other. A force seems to be trying to pull the boat straight down. The good boat is strong and has so far resisted, but I am afraid of this terrible thing. My love to you both. Simon." There, mother, you see it wasn't just the storm. But I wonder what the thing was that pulled him down.

WOMAN: Whether it was the storm or not, he is still lost to us.

TIMOTHY: But I wonder what it was that was pulling him down. It sounds so mysterious.

WOMAN: There are many mysterious things about the sea that man will never understand or be able to master, Timothy. That is why I want you to learn another trade.

TIMOTHY: Mother, I want to go down to the beach again. Perhaps I will find another message or something. Look, the storm has passed now. [*He has moved towards stage right and exits as his mother speaks.*]

WOMAN: Don't stay too long. I need you near me. [*She turns back to her chair.*] There is something very strange going on. I am afraid of it. Oh, my poor husband!
[*Curtain.*]

Scene II [*A section of the beach near the fisherman's hut. A breakwater is in the background and a few rocks are strewn about the shore. The soft sound of waves is heard all through this scene. The sea itself is not visible, but the slope of the breakwater indicates that it is somewhere at stage right. The lighting is soft, indicating late evening turning to night. Timothy enters and sits on a rock at stage centre left. He sits gazing out to sea. Then he leans forward as though looking for something.*]

TIMOTHY: [*in a soft voice*] Father! [*pause*] Father! [*Timothy stands up for a moment and then sits down again.*] I must not think about it any more. Mother is right, I must find a way to earn some money. Perhaps if I earn plenty of money I shall be able to buy a boat and go fishing again. [*He is still gazing at the sea when a ghostly-souding voice is heard singing. The voice appears to come from the sea.*]

VOICE: [*gradually getting louder*] When the high winds blow
There's us down below
Waiting, waiting, waiting
At the bottom of the sea
Blow, winds, blow!

[*Timothy at first sits still, then jumps to his feet just before the voice stops singing. On the last line of the song a strange figure enters stage right. This is the old pirate leader, Captain Blackpatch. He is dressed in traditional pirate costume, but with pieces of seaweed hanging from his clothing. The painting of his face gives a ghostly effect, which is accentuated by the stage lighting. The black patch over the left eye tends to make the face even more pale and unearthly. The Captain stops when he sees Timothy, who is too scared to move or say anything.*]

CAPTAIN: [*in a deep voice*] Well, and who is this on the shore at night, eh?

TIMOTHY: [*in a scared voice*] I . . . I . . .

CAPTAIN: Aye, aye. That's the way to answer the captain, my boy. But who are ye?

TIMOTHY: I . . . I . . .

CAPTAIN: Who are ye, boy? Answer me.

TIMOTHY: [*in shaky voice*] T . . . Timothy, sir.

CAPTAIN: Timothy, eh. Ha! Well, as for me, I'm Captain Blackpatch. I come up from the sea every now and again to visit my old haunts. This is where I and my men used to sail from before the big storm that wrecked us off the coast here. Ah, that was more than a hundred years ago. Ha, ha!

TIMOTHY: [*in awed voice*] More than a hundred years ago?

CAPTAIN: That's what I said, boy. Before your time, ha, ha! Things have changed since then, but my cave is still in the cliff up there. [*He indicates with one hand a point above and behind Timothy. Timothy half turns.*]

TIMOTHY: [*eagerly*] I know that cave, sir. It's called Blackpatch Cave. I used to play at being a pirate . . .

47

CAPTAIN: Played at being a pirate! Ha, ha! It was no play with us, boy. A very serious business, it was. It seems to have gone out of fashion these days, though. So they still call it Blackpatch Cave, eh?

TIMOTHY: Yes, sir. We fish hereabouts now . . . at least the other men do. My poor father was lost in the big storm last month and now my mother and I have to find another means to make a living.

CAPTAIN: What else can ye do, boy? Why don't ye fish too, eh?

TIMOTHY: Well, sir, when the storm took my father from us his boat was lost too, and you can't catch very many fish without a boat.

CAPTAIN: Last month, ye said, boy?

TIMOTHY: Yes, sir. Just after the full moon.

CAPTAIN: [*ruminating*] Ah, ha. What's your father's name?

TIMOTHY: He was called Simon, sir.

CAPTAIN: Simon, eh. Simon. Well, m'lad, did ye sail the seas with your father?

TIMOTHY: Yes, sir, many times. I would have been lost with him if my mother hadn't sent me to the market the day of the storm.

CAPTAIN: How would ye like to go *under* the sea for a change?

TIMOTHY: Under the sea! But that's impossible.

CAPTAIN: I spend all my time there since I was wrecked.

TIMOTHY: But I am not wrecked or drowned — at least not yet. I couldn't go under the sea.

CAPTAIN: That ye can if I take you, m'boy. I command under the sea in these parts now, just as I once did sailing on it. Will ye come?

TIMOTHY: But . . . but . . . I don't know what my mother would say.

CAPTAIN: There is no need to worry and I'll return you to this very spot. Come now. I think ye will be glad ye came.

TIMOTHY: Yes, sir, if you are sure I won't drown. If I did my mother would be completely alone.

CAPTAIN: Ye have my promise, boy. Unless ye want to stay I'll bring you back. [*The captain moves to stage right. He turns and beckons to Timothy, who slowly follows him off stage, glancing back several times as though very uncertain. As they exit the captain begins his song again.*]   When the high winds blow
There's us down below
Waiting, waiting, waiting
At the bottom of the sea
Blow, winds, blow.

[*Both the song and the sound of the waves fade as the curtain closes.*]

Scene III [*The bottom of the ocean. The background is misty with suggestions of rocks and plant life. Clumps of weeds are on each side of the proscenium. Two large rocks are in the background. A number of fish swim in and out of the scene at intervals. A pirate, Shorty John Gold, is sitting on the sea floor with his back to the largest rock. Otto, the octopus, is out of sight behind the rock.*

The sound of the captain's song is heard very faintly as the curtain opens. It gets louder. At the sound of the song, Otto waves several tentacles above the rock and one or two of them touch the pirate. The pirate makes a move to brush them away and gets to his feet.]

SHORTY: [*angrily*] Keep them arms of yours away from me, Otto. One of these days I'll get mad and tie 'em in a knot. Why the Captain wants you around I'll never know, ye useless son of a sea cook. [*The song is now louder and just as it finishes the Captain and Timothy enter from stage left. Otto's body then appears from behind the rock and he makes his way, with waving arms, towards the Captain.*]

CAPTAIN: Well, here we are. [*Timothy sees Otto and draws back.*] Don't be afraid, boy. This is Otto. I used to have a dog aboard ship, but they don't do so well down here. I suppose it is like always having a bath, eh, Shorty? Ha, ha, ha.

TIMOTHY: I've never been close to an octopus before, sir. [*Otto is bouncing gently up and down, with his tentacles moving in an undulating fashion. He embraces the Captain. Timothy is still keeping his distance.*]

CAPTAIN: Alright, down, Otto, down. [*Otto sinks to the floor. The captain turns to Timothy.*] What did you say your name was, my boy?

TIMOTHY: Timothy, sir.

CAPTAIN: Well, Timothy, meet Otto. Otto, this is Timothy. [*Otto makes a move towards Timothy, who backs off.*] Come, now, shake hands with Otto.

TIMOTHY: W-Which one, sir?

CAPTAIN: [*with roars of laughter*] Which one? Ha-ha-ha. Which one, he says. Ha-ha-ha. [*continued loud laughter. Otto briefly puts out one or two tentacles in Timothy's direction and then returns to the Captain.*] And this here, boy, is my lieutenant, Shorty John Gold. This is Timothy, Shorty.

SHORTY: Aye, aye, shipmate. [*To Captain.*] Looks a likely one for cabin boy, cap'n. When was ye wrecked, lad?

TIMOTHY: I wasn't wrecked, sir. Captain Blackpatch brought me here . . .

CAPTAIN: He isn't part of the crew, Shorty. He's a landlubber.

SHORTY: Aye, aye, cap'n, but we can soon make a seaman out of him. We got to start getting this crew together . . .

TIMOTHY: What does he mean, captain?

CAPTAIN: We're mustering another crew, boy.

49

TIMOTHY: What happened to your own crew, sir? Weren't they lost with you?

CAPTAIN: Aye, they were . . .

SHORTY: Aye, and the lazy good-for-nothing sons of sea cooks deserted us, that they did. The last of 'em went about fifty tides ago.

TIMOTHY: Why do you need a crew?

SHORTY: Every captain has a crew, don't he?

CAPTAIN: We still have a ship, boy, altho' she isn't what she used to be, what with the barnacles and every scrimshanking fish and sea urchin bunking down in her. We need a crew to get the *Marianne* shipshape again.

TIMOTHY: How will you get a crew, sir?

SHORTY: Ha, ha. We'll get a crew alright. Every storm that comes along we can press one more. We pressed one in the last storm . . .

CAPTAIN: [*interrupting hurriedly*] Avast, there, Shorty! Go and feed Otto. Here, boy, look over there and you'll see our craft. [*He points off stage right.*] It was a mighty blow that foundered the *Marianne* . . .

SHORTY: Cap'n! Let the lad feed Otto. I don't know why that lazy lump of jelly fish can't feed himself.

CAPTAIN: Belay there, Shorty. An order's an order. [*Otto, who has retired to the background, now comes forward again. He and Shorty exit stage right.*]

TIMOTHY: What did he say about the last storm, Captain?

CAPTAIN: [*embarrassed*] Nothing, lad, nothing.

TIMOTHY: I thought he said something about getting a man for the crew from the last storm . . . [*At this moment Shorty's voice is heard calling the Captain.*]

SHORTY: Ahoy, there, cap'n. Set all canvas. It's that sword again. Belay, there you . . . [*indistinguishable words and sounds of confusion off stage.*]

CAPTAIN: [*rushing off stage right*] Prepare for boarding, Shorty. I'm coming up alongside . . . [*Timothy is left alone, except for the occasional fish that swims in and out of vision. One fish is interested in him and swims up close to examine the stranger. Timothy puts a hand up to the fish and it darts away. Simon enters from stage left. He sees Timothy and stops dead.*]

SIMON: Timothy! What are you doing here? Did they drag you down in last night's storm as they did me?

TIMOTHY: [*surprised and delighted*] Father! [*They move close together.*]

SIMON: I heard the Captain shout, Tim, and came to see what was happening. I didn't expect to find you here. How is your mother, son?

TIMOTHY: Well, father, but very sad and lonely since you were lost. [*suddenly*] Father, what has happened? This is all so strange and unreal, just like a dream. I found your bottle with the message. Why were you not drowned?

50

SIMON: It wasn't the storm that put me down here, Timothy. It was the Captain and Shorty John Gold. They just pulled the boat straight down. It is here now and quite unharmed.

TIMOTHY: But, why, father? What do they want with you here?

SIMON: They have some notion that they want to get a crew together again. The crew that was wrecked with them all deserted during the years they have been down here.

TIMOTHY: But they can't sail the seas again, so why do they want a crew?

SIMON: Shorty John Gold says a captain must have men to command, but, if you want my opinion, it is really because the captain gives him all the jobs to do now that there are none of the others left. I don't think the Captain himself really minds that the men have gone, so long as he has Shorty. But tell me, son, how did you come here?

TIMOTHY: I was walking on the beach thinking about your strange message when suddenly the Captain came up from the sea, singing a song . . .

SIMON: He is always singing that song. What then, Tim?

TIMOTHY: I told him who I was and he asked me to come under the sea with him.

SIMON: Why did you come, Timothy, and leave your poor mother without either of us to look after her?

TIMOTHY: The Captain promised that, if I didn't want to stay here, he would take me back again. I believed him, father.

SIMON: The Captain is really quite a good sort, in spite of his early days. I think he will keep his word.

TIMOTHY: Since you can live in the sea, father, why didn't you try walking out the way the captain brought me here?

SIMON: I did think of it, but that Otto guards me. He seems to have as many eyes as he has legs. [looking around] I wonder where he is now? Captain Blackpatch is fonder of that ugly brute than of anything else.

TIMOTHY: The Captain told Shorty John Gold to feed Otto. Then Shorty called the Captain, saying something about a sword, and then the Captain rushed off.

SIMON: That was the big swordfish he meant. He is Otto's mortal enemy. Some day he will catch him asleep and that will be the end of Otto. [Voices are heard off stage and then the Captain and Shorty enter with Otto following from stage right.]

CAPTAIN: He got away again, Shorty, but . . . [sees Simon with Timothy] So ye are met, eh?

SHORTY: [to Simon] Why aren't ye working on them barnacles? We got to get the Marianne . . .

CAPTAIN: Let him be, Shorty, he's the lad's father.

SHORTY: [surprised] His father . . . !

CAPTAIN: Leave 'em alone a bit, Shorty. Let 'em talk. The lad might well want to stay with his father. Otto will look after them. We'll go and see how the anchor has weathered. [*The Captain and Shorty exit stage right. Otto goes to the big rock and drapes himself over it.*]

SIMON: You must not stay here, Tim; your mother needs you.

TIMOTHY: She will never believe I have seen you, father.

SIMON: You can make her believe you, son. Before you go I will give you something to prove it.

TIMOTHY: I wonder if the Captain will let me come and see you again?

SIMON: I think not, Tim, he probably thought you might want to stay here with me, but when you tell him you want to go back, you'll never see him again.

TIMOTHY: But I can't leave you here, father.

SIMON: And you can't leave your mother alone, either, Timothy. Perhaps the Captain will let me return some day. [*During this conversation both Simon and Timothy have moved as far as possible downstage.*]

TIMOTHY: Then somehow I must rescue you. If I only had your boat I could fish and wait for the chance. [*Otto is still draped over the rock. He appears to have gone to sleep.*]

SIMON: It is better that you do not go out on the sea, son, or they may drag you down in the next storm.

TIMOTHY: Why do they wait for a storm, father, they could drag boats down anytime?

SIMON: They seem to think that folks expect fishermen to be lost in a storm. They would worry more if they just disappeared. I suppose it shows that they have some thought for people. That is why I haven't given up all hope . . . [*The big Swordfish suddenly swims in from stage left. Both Timothy and Simon drop to their knees in fright. The Swordfish swims towards Otto as though to spear him. Otto suddenly becomes very much awake and waves his tentacles at the Swordfish. The Swordfish retreats and then repeatedly attacks Otto. Simon gets to his feet again.*] Stay here, son, I will get my knife from the boat. [*Simon exits stage left. The Swordfish is still attacking Otto, who is squirming about and defending himself with his tentacles. Timothy stays where he is, watching the fight. After a few moments, Simon returns with a knife in his hand. He immediately goes towards the Swordfish and joins the battle. The big fish retreats momentarily, then he attacks Simon. There is a fierce fight, but finally Simon stabs the fish with his knife and the Swordfish gradually sinks to the floor, just as the Captain and Shorty rush in from stage right. Otto seems exhausted and is lying quietly.*]

CAPTAIN: Avast there, shipmates! Who's boarding us?

TIMOTHY: [*who has risen from the floor*] The Swordfish, sir.

SHORTY: [*looking at Otto*] I knew that there sword would be the finish of Otto. [*with sarcasm*] What a terrible shame!

TIMOTHY: It didn't finish Otto, but it would have if my father hadn't killed it. [*Otto comes to life again as the Captain goes towards him.*]

CAPTAIN: [*turning to Simon*] So ye saved my Otto. Well, that was right good of you. I am fond of Otto and wouldn't want to lose him. Yes, Otto and Shorty, that's all I have to keep me company now.

SHORTY: Ah! We'll soon have a crew again, cap'n.

CAPTAIN: We don't really need a crew any more, Shorty. If we did get the *Marianne* ship-shape again, we couldn't sail the seas as we used to. We don't even need the gold any more. Shorty, ye can look after things for Otto and me. [*Loud groan from Shorty.*]

TIMOTHY: What about my father, sir?

CAPTAIN: We don't need him any more either. I'm much obliged to him for saving my Otto, so I'll send him back with you, m'boy . . .

TIMOTHY: Oh, thank you, sir, thank you. [*turns to father*] Father, you are coming back. Mother will be so happy.

SIMON: Yes, Tim, and thank you, Captain.

CAPTAIN: Well, fisherman, since ye are going back, ye might as well take your boat, too. Yes, and a present of a chest of gold. Pirates' gold. It is no use to us here. [*The Captain raises his voice.*] Bring in the fisherman's boat. [*At this command a small shoal of fish swim in with the boat suspended below them. In the boat is a chest of gold.*]

TIMOTHY: [*in surprise and delight*] Oh, thank you, Captain Blackpatch.

SIMON: I, too, thank you . . .

CAPTAIN: Don't thank me, fisherman. Just make sure that the folks on this coast don't forget that Captain Blackpatch once sailed these seas, eh, Shorty? [*Timothy and Simon board the boat.*]

SHORTY: Aye, cap'n, but don't tell 'em that Shorty John Gold now spends his time feeding a dog with eight legs. [*The fish are now carrying the boat up and out of sight as the curtain closes.*]

The Magic Book

a one act play for marionettes or hand puppets by George Merten

Characters

MOTHER	anxious about her son's indifference to books
BOBBY	her son
PROFESSOR ITSAFACT	the Chief Person in the Magic Book
MR. COMMON KNOWLEDGE	the Professor's assistant
FIGURE 1	
FIGURE 5	
FIGURE 8	all inhabitants of the Magic Book
MME. MARGUERITE	
SEMIQUAVER	
MONKEY	

Properties   Large arm chair; small chair; table; book (for the boy to read); the Magic Book.

Scene   The living room of an average home at any time.

Production notes

Although this play is primarily designed for marionettes, it can be adapted very easily for hand puppets, or for a mixture of hand and simple rod puppets.

The scene is a living room in an average home with a window upstage centre left. Furniture should include a large, comfortable chair for the boy to sit in, a small table and perhaps another chair. The large chair should be at stage left. The table can be in false perspective (narrower than it would normally be) and placed against the backdrop stage right near the window. Care must be taken that the table does not impede the movement of the characters as they emerge from the Magic Book. The other chair can be an upright chair and could be placed at stage right against the wing tab.

54

The book the boy is reading should be slightly exaggerated in size in relation to the boy. It can be propped open in a reading position on the boy's lap before the curtain opens. When he falls asleep the book can be allowed to fall to the floor and remain there throughout the rest of the play.

The Magic Book should be large. It should be about an inch or two higher than the height of the tallest puppet that emerges from it. These puppets can be of a smaller size than the scale adopted for the boy and his mother, but make sure that they are of sufficient size that they can be plainly seen by the audience. The Magic Book always remains open and, for the sake of stability when it is standing up, it would be as well to construct it rigidly in an open position. Several pages, made of stiff cardboard, can be hinged between the covers using either wire or leather for the hinges. The pages must move easily because they are turned by means of a string attached to the top corner of each page. It would help the easy turning of the pages if they were hinged just clear of the stage floor. Two or three such pages should be sufficient, otherwise there will be too many strings showing. Use a fine nylon thread for these strings in order to make them less noticeable.

The book need not have any legs or other features. Rather than try to make it appear to walk make it float through the air. This will make it less ponderous. For this animation, strings should be attached to each corner of the cover of the book.

Be sure that, when the book comes to rest, one side is just behind the wing tab at stage right. This enables the book characters to be brought on stage without being seen by the audience and they then appear to be coming directly out of the book. Remember to place the book in such position that there is room at the back for the turning of the pages. This will also ensure room for the puppets. It is a good idea to mark the book position on the floor of your stage.

The MOTHER and BOBBY should be in costume chosen in keeping with the period of the play.

PROFESSOR ITSAFACT is a kindly man with a domed forehead and a fringe of white hair. He is dressed in a classical robe which hangs quite loosely and is decorated with figures and signs, such as the signs of the Zodiac. It will be effective if the robe is of a white crush-resistant material that will hang loosely. The decoration could be in red and black.

MR. COMMON KNOWLEDGE is an old man with long, untidy white hair and a beard. He is quite a fussy type compared to the Professor. He is also dressed in a classical robe, but pale yellow in colour to offset his white hair.

THE THREE NUMERALS can be designed very simply and cut out of plywood. A suggestion of features can be incorporated into the design and defined with paint. Short legs and feet can be suspended from the figures. The figure 1 suggests a thin man. The figure 5 suggests a fat man. The figure 8 suggests a lady. The figures could be gang-strung on one control.

MADAME MARGUERITE's flower head can be made from doubled pieces of yellow felt, with a thin wire frame. The flower can be cut out in one piece, and its centre can be a half-rounded wooden button. The face is suggested merely by a set of long eye-lashes made of black leather. The centre stem can be made of wire, covered with green felt and the arms and feet of thin coiled spring wire, such as expanding wire spring curtain rods. These are twisted into position on the main stem at the shoulders and at the bottom of the stem. Large cut-out leaves of doubled green felt will make the arms and feet. When the puppet moves these will move in a springy, exaggerated manner. A bunch of green leaves, suspended downwards from the waist position forms a skirt. The veining of the leaves may be done with paint.

SEMIQUAVER, being a black note with two tails, can easily be designed into quite a bright, mischievous little puppet. He is inclined to dance about rather than walk.

The MONKEY is a simple enough character to design and make. It would be in keeping with the rest of the characters if he wore a costume.

It would be more effective if, by a system of cross fading, the stage lighting could change from white to pale blue during the dream sequence.

If it is desired to present the play using hand puppets, it is suggested that Madame Marguerite, the three figures, and Semiquaver would be effective as simple rod puppets. The design of these puppets could be much the same as suggested for the marionette figures.

The Magic Book would not float in, but it would be able to set down in a position away from the wing tab because the figures would come up behind it from below the playboard level.

The other properties would, of course, need to be adapted to the hand puppet stage.

The Magic Book

MOTHER: Well, Bobby, how much have you read? [*She bends over and looks at the book.*] Why! You are still at the same page as you were when I went out, and that was nearly an hour ago.

BOBBY: Why do I have to read books, Mother? I want to play.

MOTHER: Bobby! What a question! How will you ever learn anything if you don't read books?

BOBBY: But I don't like reading. I like to play.

MOTHER: You have never read enough to know whether you like it or not. You will never know anything about the world, or nature, or about everything else there is to know about, if you don't read.

BOBBY: The world is a long way away and I like to play better.

MOTHER: The world isn't really so far away; you only think it is because you don't read anything about it. I wonder why you always like to go out and play instead of reading sometimes.

BOBBY: Well, I suppose it is because all sorts of exciting things happen when you play — and books are just words and learning —

MOTHER: But books are exciting too. They will tell you about all kinds of things that will make your playtime all the better.

BOBBY: They couldn't do that. Playing is fun.

MOTHER: It is quite useless trying to reason with you, Bobby.

BOBBY: Can I go out and play now, Mother? The other boys will wonder where I am.

MOTHER: No, Bobby, You simply must try and read. You can't go out again to-day.

BOBBY: Aw-w, I'll just go to sleep if I have to sit here any longer.

MOTHER: Well, go to sleep then. That won't do you any harm. Look at the time! I must go back to the kitchen now and worry about supper. [*Mother exits stage right. Bobby leaves his chair and moves about stage. He goes to the window and looks out for a moment. Then he moves around again. He is grumbling about having to stay indoors.*]

BOBBY: Aw, I don't want to read. Books have nothing in them 'cept words and pages. There's no fun in books. Why can't I go out and play? [*He returns to the chair and settles in it, still grumbling.*] I don't care if I don't see another book. [*in a disgusted voice*] What will the others think if I have to stay in and read a book? [*His voice gets more sleepy as he continues to grumble. Finally he falls asleep, still muttering.*] There's nothing in books . . . [*A large animated book enters from stage right. It has a title in large letters: "Book of Knowledge". The book moves across to the boy and bends a little, as though looking at him, and then shakes a little as though in reproof. Finally it moves away and comes to rest at stage right, with one edge just out of sight behind a wing tab. It stands up in an open position with the cover to the audience. From behind the book appears the head of a genial looking old man, with a domed forehead. This is Professor Itsafact, chief person in the book. He looks around and sees the sleeping boy.*]

57

PROF. I.: So here is the boy who thinks there is nothing in books. Well, well, well. [*He emerges from behind the book and moves over to the boy, who begins to stir in his sleep.*] Perhaps we can change his mind about that. [*He leans over the boy, who looks up at that moment. He appears startled.*]

BOBBY: Who are you? Where did you come from?

PROF. I.: My name is Professor Itsafact and I came out of the Book of Knowledge. You are Bobby and you don't think there is anything in books.

BOBBY: How did you know that, Professor Itsafact?

PROF. I.: Because, like my name, it's a fact! And facts are my specialty. I must introduce you to my chief assistant, Mr. Common Knowledge. [*Prof. Itsafact moves to the book and looks around the back.*]

PROF. I.: Come out, Common Knowledge and meet the boy who doesn't think there is anything in books. [*Common Knowledge is an old man, but he is much more fussy than Prof. Itsafact. He has long, untidy white hair.*] This is Bobby, Common Knowledge, the boy who thinks there is nothing in books.

BOBBY: That is a funny name for anyone to have.

MR. C. K.: It isn't at all funny, and I would appreciate your using all of it. I hate being called just plain Common.

PROF. I.: [*to Bobby*] He is rather touchy about that, so everybody in the book is very careful. I think *you* had better be extra careful.

BOBBY: But how can you live in a book? Do others live in there too?

PROF. I.: Oh yes, thousands and thousands of others. Some are just words and figures and some are animals and plants. And then, of course, there are all the peoples of the other countries of the world, and all the inventions, like ships and trains, and just about everything you can possibly think of.

BOBBY: But what do they all do in a book?

MR. C. K.: It is really common knowledge to most people, but *you* haven't taken the trouble to find out.

PROF. I.: They tell you all about themselves, of course.

BOBBY: How do they do that?

PROF. I.: Well, it's like this. All the words and figures get together to help and they tell stories about everything.

MR. C. K.: But you have to take the trouble to read the stories if you want to find out all about things.

PROF. I.: Let me show you one or two things that are in the book, Bobby. They really are quite interesting, you know. Now, Common Knowledge, see who is on the page that is open and send them out here. [*Mr. Common Knowledge disappears behind the book. Bobby is looking from Professor Itsafact to the book in turn. He is bewildered at what is taking place.*] Now, I wonder who is on the open page. Let me see now — [*As he is speaking three animated numerals emerge from behind the book, a 1, 5 and an 8.*] Oh yes, of course, very interesting figures. [*The numerals dance around to suitable music for a few seconds and change places as they dance. When the dance and music stops, they chant in turn.*]

NO. 1: You do not know what fun is had,
Of this we are quite sure.

NO. 5: To multiply, divide, subtract and add,
Is really not a bore.

NO. 8: Or else, how will you ever know
And you certainly can't be sure. [*Bobby shows delight with the numerals.*]

BOBBY: Oh, Professor Itsafact, are all figures like that? Those I have to learn seem quite different.

PROF. I.: It is all in the way you look at them, Bobby. If you hate them, then they look back at you the same way. But if you think they are fun, then they will be fun to play with. Let me introduce you to 1, 5 and 8. [*The numerals bow.*]

BOBBY: How do you do, but where are the rest of the figures?

PROF. I.: The others are all working on a problem just now, and these three will have to go back in the book again, or they will come up with a wrong answer. [*The numerals dance back behind the book.*]

BOBBY: What else is in the book, Professor Itsafact? [*Mr. Common Knowledge puts his head out from behind the book. Professor Itsafact turns to him.*]

PROF. I.: Turn to another page please, Common Knowledge, and we'll see who is there. [*Mr. Common Knowledge disappears again and a page of the book is turned. A moment later, out comes a beautiful large yellow flower, rather like a small sunflower. It has leaves for its arms and feet, and a skirt of leaves hanging from the waist downwards.*] Ah! here we have a beautiful yellow daisy. You must meet her. This is Madame Marguerite, Bobby.

BOBBY: [*rising from his chair*] Oh! How do you do Madame Marguerite.

MADAME M.: I am very well, thank you, Bobby.

PROF. I.: What do you know about flowers, Bobby?

BOBBY: Well, they grow in the garden.

PROF. I.: Is that all you know about them?

BOBBY: I think so.

MADAME M.: What a shame. There are so many beautiful flowers in the world and they all like so much to be admired.

PROF. I.: How many flowers do you know, Bobby?

BOBBY: Well, er, let me think — there is the rose —

PROF. I.: I am afraid it is obvious that you do not know much about flowers, and that is a great pity.

MADAME M.: And to think of all the time we spend dancing in the garden to the

59

music of the wind — and you do not even notice — [*A voice is heard from inside the book.*]

VOICE: Did you say music and dancing? May I help, please? [*Out pops a little black note from the book. This is Semiquaver.*]

BOBBY: Who are you?

SEMIQUAVER: I am a Little Quaver. No music can get along without me.

PROF. I.: He really means that he is a Semiquaver.

BOBBY: That is a funny name. I've never heard of it before.

PROF. I.: There seems to be a lot of things you have never heard of before. How would you like to have Semiquaver help make some music for Madame Marguerite?

BOBBY: I would like that.

MADAME M.: Isn't that nice. I love to sway and dance, but I do not often have the opportunity when there is no wind. [*Music — Dance of the Flowers from the Nutcracker Suite. Madame Marguerite dances in imitation ballet. This should last about thirty seconds. The music stops suddenly. Madame Marguerite dances on for a moment or two longer. Then she stops. Semiquaver scurries behind the book.*]

MADAME M.: Oh dear, what has happened to the music? Where is the little note?

PROF. I.: I think he must have remembered something he had to do with the other notes. Anyway, he is back in the book.

BOBBY: What a pity!

MADAME M.: I had almost forgotten. I must get back too, or my page will be incomplete. [*Madame Marguerite dances over to the book and disappears behind it.*]

PROF. I.: Well, Bobby, I suppose I shall have to be going in a moment — [*A monkey comes out from the book and speaks to Professor Itsafact.*]

MONKEY: Professor Itsafact, Professor Itsafact, Mr. Common Knowledge sent me to tell you that it is time for the book to go back to the library. [*He looks at Bobby.*] Who is this?

PROF. I.: This is Bobby. He doesn't like books.

BOBBY: But I think I do now —

MONKEY: He is a boy. Isn't that interesting? Monkeys are descended from humans, of course.

PROF. I.: Now, you mustn't joke like that, because Bobby is getting interested in books now.

BOBBY: Do you really have to go so soon?

PROF. I.: Yes, we must, because it is nearly borrowing time again at the library and we wouldn't want to be away then in case some little girl or boy were disappointed. [*The monkey has gone back to the book and stands looking out at the Professor as though waiting for him.*]

BOBBY: Borrow? Can *I* borrow your book?

PROF. I.: Of course you can. I hope you will and then we shall all meet again. [*Bobby is sitting in the chair again and shows signs of being sleepy.*] Well, goodbye now, Bobby. I am sure we shall meet again. [*Professor Itsafact and the monkey disappear behind the book and a moment later the book goes off stage right. By this time Bobby is asleep again. After a few seconds his Mother comes back into the room. She looks at Bobby sleeping in the chair.*]

MOTHER: Bobby, wake up! [*Bobby stirs, but does not fully wake up for a moment or two.*] Bobby, wake up! [*Bobby is now awake.*]

BOBBY: Yes, mother. I am awake.

MOTHER: You fell asleep instead of reading, just as you said you would. Well, I suppose you had better go out and play if you simply won't read —

BOBBY: Mother, can anybody borrow books?

MOTHER: What did you say?

BOBBY: Can anybody borrow books?

MOTHER: Of course they can, if they go to the library.

BOBBY: Oh! Then please may I borrow a book today?

MOTHER: May *you* borrow a book! What has happened that you should want to borrow books. You don't even like reading.

BOBBY: Well, I think that what you said was right and I shall learn a lot of exciting things from books.

MOTHER: Well, who would ever have thought it? Of course you can borrow a book. Go right on down to the library. They will be open now.

BOBBY: Oh, thanks, Mother. [*Bobby goes off stage left. In a moment he returns.*]

BOBBY: Mother!

MOTHER: Yes Bobby?

BOBBY: If the other boys come and ask for me, will you tell them I shall be busy reading? [*He goes off stage left and the curtain closes as his mother stands looking after him.*]

A Little Pantomime

hand-puppet mime and dancing to the music of the suite, "The Comedians",
by Dmitri Kabalevsky (1904 -   ) by Elizabeth Merten

Characters   Two pairs of clowns, each consisting of one with a mock-serious, rather pompous face and one with a mischievous, impish face. Clowns 1 and 2 should be dressed in the same style (preferably different colours) and should have fez type hats with woollen balls, or tassels, attached by long cords to the centre-crown.

Clowns 3 and 4 also form a pair in the design of their costumes and should have tall, pointed hats with multi-coloured streamers attached to the points. (The tall hats are not fixed to the puppets' heads and should have thin elastic chin-straps to hold them on when they are worn.)

1 Ballerina in a long tutu, with long arms (preferably felt).

1 Harlequin-type clown, who is her partner.

Properties   1 small drum and drumsticks
1 pair cymbals
2 rattles, or coloured sticks with bells attached
2 fairy wands
2 candy-canes with tiny streamers at one end
1 normal-sized balloon (inflated)
1 small bouquet of flowers
Note: All the above properties, except the balloon, should be in approximately correct proportion to the size of the puppets.

Scene   The show is performed in front of a plain back-drop, to set off the bright colours of the puppets and the front curtains remain open throughout the ten short sequences of the music.

Changes of Costume   1 flimsy silk or chiffon handkerchief, ladies' size.
2 short fairy skirts or tutus open at the back, to fix on quickly with press-studs at the waists.
2 shiny stars on elastic head-bands.
1 eighteenth century powdered wig to fit Clown 4.
1 eighteenth century lady's hat to fit Clown 1.

Production notes

Due to the necessity for the inclusion of the complete working out of the details of the pantomime in the body of the script, there is little left to say by way of a production note.

The following will serve to explain the origin of a presentation of this nature and a study of the script will also serve as a guide to the working out of more of these fascinating little pantomimes.

When the audience is mainly adult or composed of older children, it will add interest to explain, by means of a programme note or verbally before the show begins, that the little pantomime is based on the tradition of the *Commedia dell' Arte*, in which a very small number of actors played a large number of parts, comic, tragic and romantic in turn, by means of minor costume changes.

Since it is hoped to draw to the attention of the audience the delightful changes of mood and rhythm in the ten sequences of the suite, the manipulators must have a quick, natural response to the music.

For the sake of clarity, the timing has been limited to the obvious bar-counts in each sequence. Details given in the choreography need not be followed exactly and are given chiefly as a guide to the kind of movements suitable for use in the different sections of the suite.

The titles of the sections are as given by the composer.

Finger cymbals, purchased in musical instrument stores, are excellent to use in the pantomime.

[The suite is used by permission of the Leeds Music Corporation.]

A Little Pantomime

1 Prologue

Clowns 1 and 2 are operated in the opening sequence by the manipulator on the left hand side. Clown 1 has the cymbals fixed in his hands; Clown 2 has the drum [fastened round his neck by tie-strings] and the drumsticks in his hands.

a After two introductory bars [*during which the front curtains open*] Clown 1 appears at stage left and starts to clash his cymbals in correct tempo and to parade back and forth along the playboard, returning to extreme stage left as the first half of the melody finishes.

b Clown 2 appears at stage right and beats his drum and parades for the second half of the melody, while Clown 1 watches, miming surprise, not playing.

c Clown 1 resumes playing as the melody is repeated, but is interrupted after eight clashes by Clown 2, who beats the drum eight times.

d Clown 1 makes four clashes; Clown 2 makes four bangs.

e Clown 1 makes two clashes; Clown 2 makes two bangs.

f They clash and bang alternately, as though arguing musically, until just before the end of this musical section, when they turn inwards to face each other, advance to meet in the centre, now playing simultaneously, collide and disappear quickly down below the playboard on the final note.

2 Gallop

The right-hand-side manipulator is ready with Clowns 3 and 4, who have rods or rattles attached to their outside hands, i.e. right-hand puppet to the right hand, left-hand puppet to the left hand. After a short musical introduction, on the first bar of the melody the puppets begin to rise from below the centre of the playboard, with arms outstretched and inside hands touching, as follows:

a Eight small upward jerks in rhythm to the first eight counts of the melody, the points of the hats showing on the first count and only the heads and arms by the time the eighth count is reached. For the next eight counts they pause in their upward movement and shake their bells, or rattles, four times.

b Repeat **a** for the next sixteen counts of the melody, finishing with the puppets fully extended above playboard.

c Take four counts to separate the puppets to right and left and the next sixteen to bring them down slowly, in dipping and circling movements [*by circling movements of the manipulator's wrists*] to below playboard level, where they are quickly drawn together to their original position, ready to rise again.

d Repeat **a** and **b**.

e This time there are only twelve counts available to be used for descent, before the contrasting melody begins. One puppet turns inward and bends at the waist to look below, taking four counts — the other puppet imitates this, taking another four counts — and both are drawn down out of sight in this position [*another four counts*].

64

f In the contrasting melody which now begins, the pointed hats of the clowns pop up and down alternately in time to the music, moving in turn to the far right and left of the playboard respectively and back towards the centre again. [*Two counts each time and taking care not to show more than the hats.*]

g For the short bridge-passage which leads back to the main melody, the two clowns' heads are shaken vigorously on the manipulator's hands, still at the same level, to give lots of movement to the streamers at the points of the hats. Just before the re-entrance of the melody, the heads disappear quickly, ready to resume opening positions.

h Repeat **a**, **b** and **c**.

i The final 32 counts of the melody have now been reached. During the first eight bring Clown 4 up as though climbing over the back of the playboard, during the second eight repeat this with Clown 3; during the last sixteen counts they turn inwards smartly, one after the other, bow in turn to each other, then face front again and dance out in opposite directions.

3 March

During the "Gallop" section, the left-hand-side manipulator has had time to remove the cymbals, drum and drumsticks from Clowns 1 and 2.

a As the music of this sequence begins, Clown 1 puts his head in stealthily from stage left, looks round to see if the coast is clear, puts a finger to his lips, disappears and re-appears bearing the drum, which he carries to centre-stage and lays down. These actions occupy sixteen counts, the first half of the melody.

b The rest of the melody is used for a little dance of triumph round the drum, bending from the waist and tapping it with one hand, then the other, in the rhythm of the tune, straightening and clapping his hands, jumping round in delight to finish on the right-hand side of the drum.

c As the contrasting section of the melody begins [*the third sixteen counts*] Clown 2 appears from stage right, bending and straightening himself in staccato movements which fit the music, looking everywhere for his drum, first outside the playboard, then down into the well of the stage, in turn.

d During this action, Clown 1 stretches himself as far as he can in front of the drum to hide it and after eight beats moves forward, nods, turns Clown 2 around, points out to right, beyond the front of the open curtain, and both look out there. This takes another eight counts.

e Clown 2 goes on peering out to the right, while Clown 1 steals away, picks up the drum and takes it away, off stage left. Another eight counts.

f During the final eight counts of the melody, Clown 2 straightens himself, turns round and sees that his friend has gone, turns back and stares puzzled at the audience, puts a hand to his chin and rubs it, nods and hides behind right curtain, popping his head out once and in again as the music stops.

4   Waltz

As soon as Clown 1 has departed from the previous scene, the right-hand-side manipulator takes him off his partner's left hand and substitutes the ballerina. On her hands are pinned the diagonally opposite ends of the silk square — this should be done before the show begins. After she has made her appearance in this sequence, Clown 2 is changed from the right hand of this puppeteer to the right hand of his partner, who makes him look out from the right curtain once or twice during her dance, as though watching with surprise and delight. After four introductory counts or bars, the ballerina appears at stage left and, facing the front with her arms forward —

a sways sideways from the waist twice to the right and twice to the left, in rhythm, dipping the head over to the same side each time. This movement is repeated to the end of the first section of the melody, moving the puppet along the playboard and back.

b With the puppet still facing the front, the manipulator makes two circling movements forward with his wrist, then pushes his arm over to the extreme right end of playboard, palm of hand facing diagonally outwards and puppet-arms outstretched, allowing movement of the scarf. This gives the impression that the dancer is circling from the waist and then taking a graceful leap out to the right. The same movements are repeated to the left, taking four counts in all.

c The puppet is swept from side to side of the playboard four times to four counts, with a forward dip of the wrist at centre stage each time, ending each sweep with the same upward pose as before and holding it the last time for two counts.

d **b** and **c** are then repeated and the last four counts of this first half of the sequence are used to bring the dancer to centre-stage, bend her forward from the waist as far as the wrist will go, with arms fully outstretched, then dip the head inside the extended scarf and turn the wrist round to straighten up with the puppet facing the back-curtain and the scarf extended behind her back.

e As the melody begins again **a** is repeated with the puppet's back to the audience and arms outstretched this time. After sixteen counts, bending the body of the puppet back from the waist, use the next and final sixteen counts to move it in a wide, slow semi-circle from right to left of the playboard and back, with the scarf fluttering between the outstretched arms; raise the puppet by straightening the wrist again to a standing position, turn her to face the front, draw the hands close together for a second and then finish in a curved leap off stage to the left, with arms outstretched, and scarf still behind her back.

5 Pantomime

This sequence is manipulated by the right-hand-side puppeteer, who is now ready with Clowns 1 and 2 on his left and right hands. This gloomy little piece is used to mime the despairing love of Clown 2 for the ballerina he has just seen, the consternation of Clown 1 at his friend's tears, which he attempts in vain to dry by bringing back the drum stolen in the third sequence and his final sympathy for his friend's unhappiness.

a Clown 2 appears from the right curtain on the first count and walks from right to left of the playboard in slow rhythm to the music, head hanging forward, hands up to eyes, for eight counts.

b He turns to the front and stands there for eight counts, looking up with arms outstretched and looking down with hands to face alternately.
a is then repeated, moving back to right side of stage, where **b** is repeated.

c As the melody begins again, he remains there, head down, with the tassel or ball on his hat swinging forward in front of him, while Clown 1 enters from stage left, popping his head in first, catching sight of the despondent Clown 2, miming concern as he moves over and tries to look into his face, pushing the tassel away and lifting it back and letting it swing down again several times — a second sixteen counts.

d Clown 2 keeps pushing him away and turning away from him. At last Clown 1 has an inspiration and goes off to left [*eight counts*], returning with the drum which he carries across and sets down on playboard near his friend — eight counts. He taps him on the shoulder and he looks up and stares at the drum, then pushes it with a sweep of his arm right off the playboard [*inside the well of the stage*], as though he didn't want it any more. Clown 1 then puts his arm comfortingly around his friend and pats him. They go off to stage left together as the music finishes — eight counts.

6 Intermezzo

During the previous sequence, the left-hand-side manipulator has had time to put the fairy skirts round the waists of Clowns 3 and 4, replaced their hats with the starry head-bands and placed wands in their hands. They are on his hands ready to begin.

a Clown 4 comes in from stage left facing front and hops across the playboard to right side and out, moving in thirty-two tiny hops, like a tiptoing movement.

b For the next thirty-two counts this is repeated by Clown 3, who then hops back to centre-stage, followed by Clown 4.

c They turn after eight counts and face each other, bowing alternately [*eight counts*] and as the melody recommences they do a little dance, advancing and retiring twice [*sixteen counts*], then hopping past each other and back twice [*by crossing the wrists right in front of left, then left in front of right*] for sixteen counts. They face the front, inside hands touching, bow together to the audience, and slowly drop below the playboard at centre-stage as music ends.

7 Little Lyrical Scene

This section is in slow waltz tempo. At the beginning the ballerina [on the left hand of the left-hand-side manipulator] appears from left curtain, hands crossed demurely in front.

a For eight counts she walks across stage to right and back to left, looking around as though she is waiting for someone.

b She leans against the left curtain, gazing out front dreamily, while from stage right Clown 2, still on the right hand of the right-hand-side manipulator, enters, mimes delighted surprise, approaches her, bows, tries to attract her attention, gives her a little pat, whereupon she looks round and slaps his face, so he goes away again to stage-right, crestfallen. This action occupies the next sixteen counts to the end of the melody.

c As it recommences, Clown 2 returns, carrying a bouquet which he offers to her. She is melted and takes it into her own hands, then bends forward and kisses the clown. This takes up the first sixteen counts of the repeat melody.

d At the seventeenth count [*an emphatic point in the music*] they are caught in the act by the harlequin who comes up quickly from below behind the pair [*on left-hand side puppeteer's right hand*] and forces himself between them, chases Clown 2 away and off stage and returns to take the bouquet from the lady and cast it dramatically down behind the playboard.

e The last sixteen counts of this little sequence, which are in the nature of a coda or finishing-off piece, are used for harlequin to move over to stage right, miming righteous indignation, and for the little lady to mime tears and entreaties as she follows him over. There is a final tender reconciliation as they are drawn gently down below the playboard at the last count, with their arms round each other.

8 Gavotte

Clown 1 now has an eighteenth century period hat fitted over his own hat, with the tassel pushed up into the crown. This has been done by the right-hand-side manipulator during the Intermezzo sequence and during the latter part of the Little Lyrical Scene he has had time to take off the fairy skirt and head-band from Clown 4 and put on an eighteenth century powdered wig. He is ready to bring these two puppets up at centre, Clown 1 on his left hand and Clown 4 on his right, as the gavotte-music starts. During this little sequence the puppets should imitate gavotte-movement as far as possible and always move in strict tempo. They appear together at centre stage, well back from the playboard, inside arms touching and extended.

a They take two steps diagonally forward to left [*to one count of four beats*] with heads inclined to left; the same to right, then repeat to each side.

b Repeat **a** moving backwards for four counts.

c The puppets separate and repeat the same movement diagonally out to left and right ends of playboard [*four counts*]; advance to meet each other along the playboard [*four counts*], finishing by the gentleman bowing to his partner and the lady dropping down in a supposed curtsey.

Here there is a hesitation in the music and the gentleman turns his back on the audience and gives the lady his inside hand, so that his right and her right are touching and extended.

d As the contrasting melody begins, they move round, doing the same "step", the lady to the right, gentleman to the left, in a semi-circle, taking two counts, and move back in tempo to their original positions for two counts. This is repeated and on the last beat the inside hands are changed and the movement is repeated again in the opposite direction for two more counts.

e They part and move outward, facing each other, towards the ends of the playboard [*two counts*] and move back in again, bowing and curtseying at centre and getting themselves into position for the final part of the routine, by the lady turning her back on the audience and extending her left hand to touch the gentleman's left.

f As the first melody begins again, the lady ducks her head down under the extended touching arms and comes up in front of the gentleman. They move to the right, dipping their arms to right and left alternately for four counts.

g She withdraws her head in the same way, bringing it back again under the two touching left arms and straightens up again with her back to the audience; bends back from the waist and as she does so the gentleman bends his head over to the left as though looking into her face and then straightens again — another four counts. This part of the routine, from **f** to **g** is repeated and at the end the puppets bow and curtsey once more and are drawn down below at centre.

9   Scherzo

This sequence is on similar lines to the Waltz (4) but much faster, giving the impression of graceful ballet as far as possible. During the Gavotte, the left-hand-side manipulator has put the ballerina [without scarf] on his left and the harlequin on his right hand.

a   As the music begins, the ballerina appears from stage left, whirling from the waist three times, and leaping diagonally upwards to extreme stage right on the fourth count.

b   She moves in a dipping curve to the same pose at stage left, then to right, then to left, then to right [*four more counts*], extending arms at the highest point of each curve.

c   From this position she does a back-bend, two counts back and two up, moves quickly to stage left and repeats this, bending diagonally to the left again. **a** and **b** are then repeated and during the last four counts on this melody she faces front and takes four similar, but smaller, leaping upwards movements to the left, the fourth leap taking her completely off stage.

d   As the contrasting melody begins, the harlequin enters from stage right. He claps his hands on the first count, throws himself back from the waist in a back-bend, with arms wide, on the second count, and repeats these two actions four times to the left, then four times to the right, taking sixteen counts.

e   He then faces front and swings over sideways from the waist eight times to eight counts to left and right [*manipulator's wrist bending over from side to side*], gradually moving across stage to left at the same time.

f   He uses the last eight counts of this section to do eight back-bends facing left and moving back to stage right and out on the last count, clapping his hands together and throwing them apart between each.

g   As the opening melody recommences, the ballerina repeats her routine from **a** to **c** again, until the last eight counts, when the harlequin appears from stage right and kisses her hand gallantly.

h   As the contrasting melody is repeated, both puppets repeat from **d** to **f** until the last four counts, when they turn in to face each other and the lady does her last four back-bends going in the opposite direction. Neither goes off stage this time and, as the ballerina's melody comes in for the third time, she starts her routine again. Her partner is waiting for her at extreme stage right and catches her with his arms on her waist at the fourth count, pushing her up in ballet-style. He then follows her to and fro across stage as she repeats **b**, catching her each time she pauses. As she repeats **c** he bends over with an arm below her waist and looks into her face. The same action from **a** to **b** is repeated once more, and the last four counts are used for a deep bow and curtsey as the puppets are drawn down below the playboard.

70

10 Epilogue

During the previous sequence, the right-hand-side manipulator has put the original hats back on Clowns 3 and 4 and placed the candy-canes in their outside hands. He has also taken the period hat off Clown 1 and left Clowns 1 and 2 ready to be put on the left-hand-side manipulator's hands, as soon as he has discarded the puppets from the "Scherzo" sequence.

a Clowns 3 and 4 do a gay dance on their own, appearing at centre as soon as the introduction is over, waving the streamers on the canes to and fro in time to the music. For the first sixteen counts they move gradually away from each other to opposite ends and back to the centre again.

b For the second sixteen counts they turn in to face each other. Clown 4 tickles the face of Clown 3 with the streamers on the cane for four counts, while Clown 3 turns away, then Clown 4 stretches over to reach his turned-away face and tickles him again. By the eighth count they are facing each other again and the same movement is repeated with Clown 3 taking the offensive. It is then repeated once again by Clown 4, then by Clown 3, and after that they start to belabour one another with the canes.

c As they are doing this, Clowns 1 and 2 appear from the left curtain, hurry along the playboard and stop the fighting by pulling the sticks out of their friends' hands and dropping them down behind the playboard. This brings us to a hesitation in the music before the next melody begins and the four puppets use this to get into a circle at centre-stage, with all their outspread arms touching.

d As the new melody begins, all four move in eight little hops round in one direction, then eight times back, and repeat both ways. Then four hops one way and four hops back and repeat; two hops each way and two back, repeat, and finally spread out in a long line and hop twice to the right and twice to the left to the end of the melody, when Clowns 3 and 4 separate themselves and go out quickly to the right — this whole routine occupying sixteen counts altogether.

e Clowns 1 and 2, now on stage alone, lean their heads well out over the front of the playboard and swing the tassels on the hats round in circles outside the proscenium, the puppets moving away from each other to the ends of the playboard and then back to centre again [*eight counts*] and, as a big crescendo begins in the music, they stop, look down into the well of the stage, look up again and clap their hands with joy; move to the left side of the stage, Clown 1 forward, facing inwards to the right and Clown 2 facing in the same direction but well back, near the back-curtain, both with arms outspread.

f As the final melody begins, Clowns 3 and 4 come up from below, bearing a normal-sized balloon between them [*hung by a loose loop and a long, thin thread round the neck of one of them*] and they throw it to Clowns 1 and 2, who throw it back again, and so on to the end of the music, throwing on each count. Just before the end, the four puppets press the balloon against the point of a pin which has been set, before the show began, in a place on the centre front of the playboard where it has not been able to do any damage, and after it bursts on the final notes, all puppets put their hands up to their faces and duck down behind.

[*Curtain*]

The Boy with Green Fingers

a play for puppets in two acts by Elizabeth Merten

Characters:

Mistress Jones	
Gary 'Greenfingers' Jones	A young boy (about ten years old, with red hair, green eyes and green-painted hands)
A witch	
Master Potts	An old gardener
A Sergeant	
A Corporal	
A Princess	

Scene   The interior of a country cottage.

Act. I — rather dim and shadowy lighting with an effect of firelight if possible; in this act there is a cradle on stage.

Act II — bright lighting, giving an effect of sunlight. The set has two windows with tall flowers growing outside; there is a table with a bowl of flowers in the room.

Properties   A cradle

A table, with a bowl of flowers and an open book on it

A scroll

A flower-pot containing a plant

Music   Folk-tunes, for opening, entr'acte and closing

15 minutes   two manipulators

Production notes

These notes are not intended to dictate the exact way the play should be produced, but are included as a guide to the various possibilities and the treatments that could be used. Every producer should bring as much individuality as possible to a production.

The play was written for hand puppets, but a stronger impact will be obtained in Act I if the witch is a hand and rod puppet. Before the witch actually appears on the stage, she can be given an effective build-up by lighting and shadows, and by suitable music; when she appears she can have long arms and flowing draperies. This will help create a feeling of impending evil and the witch's pronouncements will be all the more effective, particularly if the voice is well cast. This treatment would also strengthen the character, who, by casting a spell, provides the whole basis for the plot, but has only one brief appearance.

The characters

The Witch, as already suggested, would be more striking if she is a hand and rod puppet. The head modelling should be strong and well defined. Be careful not to reduce the strength of the features when painting the head. Remember this character appears only in a faintly-lit room. Make the under-glove and the flowing draperies of the costume exceptionally long, so that the figure can appear to fly rather than walk. The hand control wires should be correspondingly long.

The Baby is not seen, and only heard briefly, in Act I; being tucked up in the depths of the cradle.

Mistress Jones should be a normally pleasant character dressed in the story-book costume of a country woman, with, perhaps, a mob cap.

Mr. Potts is a kindly old man with a weatherbeaten face and white hair. Such accessories as spectacles or a moustache could be considered. Some part of his costume could be a faded green colour.

Gary 'Greenfingers' Jones is described in the play as 'ugly'. This should be an appealing ugliness, not the repulsive type. Considerable care should be given to achieving this effect since he is the chief character in the play.

The two Soldiers should be in typical toy-soldier costumes, with three and two stripes respectively.

The Princess is young and beautiful and dressed in pink or blue, as story-book princesses invariably are.

The set and properties

The full effect of the setting will depend largely on the type of stage used. If the background is painted on a scrim, then it is merely a question of showing two windows with perhaps a dresser and chair also painted in. The cradle can be clipped to the back edge of the playboard. However, some consideration should be given, in addition to the replacing of the cradle by a table in Act II, to the passing of ten years. This could be effected by a quick change of scrims during the brief curtain between the acts. (This interval should be counted in seconds, not minutes!) The scrim for the opening scene could, for instance, have closed shuttered windows and other characteristics that would assist in the creation of the desired atmosphere.

The general lighting should be dim, as though from an oil lamp, but there should be sufficient light in which to play the scene without appreciably increasing it after Mistress Jones' entrance.

The scrim for Act II would have the windows in exactly the same positions as for the opening scene, but they would be open to bright sunlight with tall flowers growing outside.

The bowl of flowers should be fastened to the table. This makes one instead of two properties to position in a short space of time and also eliminates the possibility of the bowl being knocked over or displaced.

If desired, the backgrounds could be merely 'draped', in which case it would be more effective to use two different colours of scrim type material that could be changed in the way suggested above. This treatment would give a distinct change of atmosphere and time to the two scenes. A dark blue or dark grey for the first act and either a medium grey or soft light brown for Act II would be suitable.

If the play is to be given on a stage where the puppets are held higher than the operator's head then the setting should be designed to the full depth of the stage. One or two wing drapes, or tabs, will give the witch more scope for movement. She might flit from one tab to another and peer around before finally approaching the cradle and uttering the fateful curse.

With this type of stage two added effects could be gained if the garden scene were set back nine to twelve inches behind the window set. This could also effect an economy in the setting as the windows could have movable shutters which could be closed during the first act and opened on the pre-set garden scene for the second act. The lighting here would also be effective if it were dim behind the shuttered windows and increased to bright sunlight in the second act. An effect might also be gained by some movement of the closed shutters prior to the entrance of the witch.

The soldiers and the princess could be made to pass by the windows before entering. If you do this, remember they should pass by again after their exits.

If the stage area is large enough, consideration might be given to the use of a well-ballasted pedestal that reaches to the eye-level of the playboard. Both the cradle and the table could be clipped to this in turn. More effects can be gained if the puppets can move all round these properties.

Whatever treatment and colour schemes are involved in the production, work all this out before designing the costumes. The characters must always stand out from the backgrounds, not be overwhelmed by them. In a well-balanced stage design the characters and backgrounds should complement each other and, with careful study beforehand, the colours used can become as integral a part of the presentation as can music, for instance. This does not mean that the colours used should 'match'; violent clashes of the right colours can greatly assist the dramatic effects if they are the *right* colours. Do not neglect the possibility of dyeing materials if you cannot buy the colours suitable for your purpose.

The Boy With Green Fingers

Act one

[*As curtain opens, Witch enters from stage left, looks around and creeps in a sinister fashion across stage towards cradle, cackling as she goes.*]

WITCH: Ah-hah! A new baby, I see! Nobody watching it either — here's a chance for me. Ha-ha! Nothing I enjoy so much as casting a spell over a new baby! [*She cackles and crouches over cradle.*] May you be so stupid and ugly that everyone will laugh and be unkind to you all your miserable life! [*She laughs in a cracked voice and gloats over the cradle. The baby cries.*]

[*Mrs. Jones enters from stage left, sees the witch and screams in horror.*]

WITCH: [*triumphantly*] The spell is cast. Too late! Too late!

[*She cackles as she flies off and exits stage right.*]

MRS. JONES: Oh, my poor baby! What has that dreadful witch done to you? Oh dear, what shall I do? Your life will be ruined from the start, if I can't find some way of breaking the spell. Oh dear! Oh dear!

[*Master Potts, the old gardener, enters from stage right. He peers at Mrs. Jones.*]

POTTS: You sound terrible upset, Mistress Jones — what's the matter?

MRS. JONES: Oh, Master Potts, I heard the baby cry just now and when I came into the room I saw a horrible witch bending over the cradle. She flew away as fast as lightning, but she had already laid a wicked spell on my son. [*Mrs. Jones sobs.*]

POTTS: Dear me, that's very serious, to be sure. Now let me think what's to be done. [*He scratches his head and thinks for a moment.*] I'm only an old gardener, of more use to the flowers than to human beings . . . but there's one thing I can do for him. May I touch the baby, Mistress Jones, just for a moment? You know I wouldn't hurt the little fellow.

MRS. JONES: Yes, yes, do anything that might help to break the spell . . . what are you going to do?

[*Master Potts crosses to cradle and touches the baby. He then stands up straight and speaks proudly.*]

POTTS: Now come and look at your child.

MRS. JONES: [*going to cradle and bending over*] Master Potts! What have you done, you stupid old man? What's that green stuff on his hands . . . as though things weren't bad enough already. Take it off this instant . . . hurry, you idiot!

POTTS: [*hurt but dignified*] So you don't appreciate my gift to the baby! Don't you know what having green fingers means?

MRS. JONES: Whoever heard of such a thing? Take it off at once.

POTTS: Once the gift of green fingers is given, it can never be taken back again.

MRS. JONES: [*horrified*] What?

POTTS: You don't understand . . . it means that your son will have a power over plants and flowers that will seem like magic . . . nothing will ever fail to grow for him.

MRS. JONES: Well, that's a great consolation, I must say.

POTTS: I thought it might be something to make the poor boy happy — just to be able to grow lovely flowers. If he is going to have other unpleasant things to face in his life, just think of the pleasure of looking at a perfect rose.

MRS. JONES: Perfect fiddlesticks! Now my poor child has to go through life with goodness knows what evils dogging his footsteps — and green fingers besides! If that's all you can do, Master Potts, go away at once and never come into this cottage again.

[*She turns her back on him.*]

POTTS: [*angrily*] And not a word of thanks! Oh well, you'll see, you ungrateful woman. One day when I am dead and gone you will wish you had said a thank-you to this crazy old man. Just you wait and see.

[*Mrs. Jones laughs scornfully, still with her back to him.*]

POTTS: You wait and see.

[*Master Potts exits stage right. Mrs. Jones turns and bends over the cradle again as the curtain closes and music begins.*]

Act two

[*As music fades and curtain opens, Gary "Greenfingers" Jones, a boy of ten, is at a table looking at a book. A bowl of flowers on the table attracts his attention and he touches the flowers gently. Mrs. Jones enters from stage right in time to see the gesture.*]

MRS. JONES: Gary! Get on with your lessons. What page are you at now?

GARY: Page one.

MRS. JONES: That's disgraceful — you're a lazy and useless boy. Read me the first sentence at the top of page two.

GARY: [*haltingly*] The boy — said — I wish — I was — in the garden — where — the grass is green — and soft — and — the sun —

MRS. JONES: [*interrupting*] Gary! You're making that up. It's not in the book at all, you bad boy.

[*Gary shakes with laughter.*]

MRS. JONES: No, it's not funny, Gary. Read me what is there, if you please, and stop plaguing your poor widowed mother.

GARY: [*sighing deeply*] But I'm only interested in flowers, not in books. What's the use of having green fingers if you won't let me use them?

MRS. JONES: I'm waiting . . . Oh, how I wish that Master Potts had kept his gift to himself.

GARY: [*sighing again*] The cat — sat — on the . . .

MRS. JONES: [*looking out of the window*] Gracious me, there's a great big carriage outside and a soldier coming up the path. I wonder what he wants?

[*Gary turns and goes to look too. He becomes excited.*]

GARY: Isn't it exciting, mother?

[*A sergeant enters from stage left, carrying in his hands an opened scroll, from which he reads.*]

SERGEANT: Silence, good people all, and listen to the Royal Pronouncement.

[*Gary and Mrs. Jones bow and stand close together, listening.*]

SERGEANT: Somewhere in this village there is known to be a young male person who is said to be very ugly and stupid.

[*Gary and Mrs. Jones turn and look at each other, then listen again.*]

SERGEANT: He is quite small and has red hair and green eyes. He is a very bad scholar and has a mischievous character.

[*Gary hides behind Mrs. Jones and as the following speech finishes he makes for the exit stage right.*]

SERGEANT: All good citizens are required to assist in the finding of this person and the search will continue until he is found, by order of His Majesty.

[*He stops reading and spots Gary, about to disappear.*]

SERGEANT: Hey! come back here . . . where d'you think you're going? [*He takes a good look at Gary.*] Well, what d'you know — just a minute now. [*He pulls Gary back to centre-stage.*] Red hair, green eyes . . . ugly . . . h'm, h'm . . . and green fingers too! I'm blest if you're not the very one we're looking for.

MRS. JONES: [*very agitated*] Oh, sir, he's my only son. What has he done? He is indeed ugly and stupid and mischievous . . . but he's all I've got, General.

SERGEANT: [*clearing his throat*] Er, h'm — not a general yet, madam, just a sergeant.

MRS. JONES: And a very fine one you look too.

SERGEANT: Thank you, madam.

MRS. JONES: Please may I speak to my son before you take him away?

SERGEANT: Oh well, I don't see any harm in that, but don't be long now.

MRS. JONES: What have you been up to, Gary?

GARY: N-n-nothing, mother . . . nothing at all. There must be a mistake.

MRS. JONES: There must be a mistake, Sergeant.

SERGEANT: I don't think so, madam, but we can soon find out. [*Shouts in his army voice.*] Corporal!

[*They all look towards off-stage left. Corporal enters, bearing a flower-pot with the top of a very sorry-looking plant showing in it.*]

SERGEANT: [*to Gary*] Now then, my lad. We, that is, the Royal Family and myself, have been hearing some remarkable things about you. This extremely rare foreign plant [*he gestures towards the Corporal*] is the pride and joy of the Crown Princess and, as you can see, it is withering away. All the — hrmphm, hrmphm — horti- horti- horticultural experts — [*aside*] that means the best gardeners, I suppose — have tried in vain to revive it, and the Princess is very upset and worried. In fact, I declare she is fading away too. So here's your chance, my boy — if you really have the powers we've heard about, give this plant a new lease of life and your fortune will be made. If you can't . . . well, let me see . . . p'raps you'd make a good soldier . . . yes, if you fail, we'll recruit you for the army.

MRS. JONES: Oh no . . . please don't take him away.

SERGEANT: Now then, Corporal — three paces forward M-A-R-R-CH! Halt! Now then, Master Gary Greenfingers — it's up to you. Proceed.

[*Gary approaches the pot and strokes the plant.*]

GARY: [*softly*] Poor plant . . . poor lonely plant . . . far away from your own country . . . you just need a little affection, don't you . . .

[*Slowly the plant rises above the level of the rim of the pot and blossoms appear on the stalk. It should rise a good way above the head of the Corporal. Gary shows it to the Sergeant and moves closer to his mother again. The Sergeant comes forward and inspects it closely.*]

SERGEANT: [*in wonder*] Well, if I hadn't seen that happen, I wouldn't have believed it. That's the most wonderful thing I ever saw . . . now you will be rewarded for your cleverness. Just wait till the Princess sees it. Take it out to the carriage, Corporal, and show it to Her Highness.

[*The Corporal carries the plant out stage left.*]

MRS. JONES: [*excitedly*] The Princess is here? [*Gary turns and looks out of the window.*]

GARY: Oh, mother, isn't it thrilling — we'll never forget this day, shall we?

SERGEANT: [*roaring*] Attention, everyone.

[*All stand stock still. The Princess enters from stage left. She is young and beautiful.*]

PRINCESS: Where is the person who gave my plant back its life and beauty?

SERGEANT: [*to Gary*] Three paces forward — MARCH.

PRINCESS: [*extending a hand, as Gary bows*] We are proud to have you among our subjects. There are few with such a wonderful gift as yours. I appoint you here and now Head Gardener to the Palace for the rest of your life.

[*Mrs. Jones gasps for joy.*]

GARY: I can never thank you enough, Your Highness.

PRINCESS: Is this your mother?

MRS. JONES: Welcome to our humble cottage, Your Highness. Your presence is a very great honour for us, Your Highness.

PRINCESS: Your home may be humble, but all these flowers make it a place of beauty. You must be proud of your clever son.

MRS. JONES: Indeed I am, Your Highness.

PRINCESS: Fare you well then, but see that he arrives at the Palace early tomorrow to take over his duties.

[*Gary and Mrs. Jones bow low as the Princess exits stage left, followed by the Sergeant.*]

MRS. JONES: Gary Greenfingers Jones, you wonderful, clever, darling boy.

GARY: Hurray, hurray!

[*They hug each other, then Mrs. Jones looks at Gary seriously.*]

MRS. JONES: But there's one thing we must not forget, Gary.

[*He nods in agreement and they turn to the front, raise their faces skywards and say very solemnly in unison.*]

GARY AND MRS. JONES: [*together*] Thank you, Master Potts.

[*As curtain closes, soft folk-tune concludes the show.*]

A Head for Peppino

a play for hand puppets by George Merten

Characters:

Peppino	A boy puppet with red hair and a longish, uptilted nose and bright eyes. The head is not fastened to the costume, but may be removed as necessary from the forefinger to allow the substitution of other heads.
	Peppino has two extra heads — a dog's head and a cannibal's head with a bone through the nose. Both heads have bright red hair.
Magician	Dressed in traditional robes, but not a frightening character. He has a domed forehead, is benevolent and somewhat absent-minded.
Blinkie	A clown
	A narrator reads the prologue
Scene	This play can very well be done in drapes, but if scenery is desired then it could be set in either a puppet workshop or back stage in a hand puppet theatre.
Properties	A stage mirror, a light screen, large enough to conceal a puppet adequately.

about 15 minutes   two or three manipulators

Production notes

Two things in particular are of extreme importance to the success of this play — the timing and an imaginative voice for the Magician. There is ample scope for pantomime and for good acting generally. It will be found effective if the narration is given over very soft background music, but the music will need to be chosen with great care because at no point must it predominate. To this end the music should maintain a fairly constant level of sound and should be faded as the curtain opens. Study the play carefully, particularly with regard to the timing of the entrances and exits during the spell sequences. Once Peppino has appeared wearing in turn each of the two extra heads, it is unnecessary to use the puppet body when these heads appear round the side of the screen, either separately or together.

The play can be given with two manipulators, but three will enable more character to be given to each role. In any case, considerable rehearsal will be necessary to effect a smooth flow of movement.

The characters

All three puppets should have as long arms as possible, but still retain the ability to handle the properties as necessary. Felt covered wire hands are recommended.

Peppino should be quite amusing, but also attractive. His hair should be as red as possible. For the best effect, theatrical crêpe hair is suggested.

Take care that all three heads fit snugly on the finger, otherwise they may drop off at the wrong moment.

It is not essential that his nose should be long, but it will assist to make the character amusing, but not necessarily ugly.

The red hair should be a distinctive feature of the other two heads since this provides the common denominator.

Great care should be taken that the Magician is an amiable character, both in appearance and manner. His robes could be decorated with the usual symbols associated with magicians, but avoid anything of a frightening nature, otherwise the character will be inconsistent with the magician of the play. No mention is made of a wand, but one may be used if desired.

Blinkie is an ordinary circus clown. If his eyes are crossed with a plus (+) sign, it will assist to point up his name. Care should be taken that no part of his costume impedes his handling of the properties.

The setting

Drapes are suggested as the background for the play, but be careful to make the drape and costume colours complementary. The puppets should not be absorbed by the background. In planning this, take into account the extra heads to be used in the play.

The properties

There are only two properties other than the extra heads — the mirror and the screen. The mirror should not be a real mirror (that would be contrary to theatrical tradition), but a painted mirror set up on a firm, flat base. The mirror itself is never seen by the audience. The screen must be of light-weight material because the clown has to hold it up for quite a long time. It can have some suitable design painted on it, but this should not be over-elaborate, otherwise it will detract from the heads that are poked out from it. It must be large enough to conceal Peppino and also the manipulator's two hands when the heads are used separately from the body.

Lighting

The lighting will be more effective if dimmers are available. White light, with perhaps some pink or blue added to tone it down in brightness, will create more 'atmosphere'. The lights should fade with the drawing of the final curtain.

A head for Peppino

NARRATOR: Peppino is a puppet. He hasn't been a puppet very long because the puppet-maker has only just finished him. Peppino has spent most of his life so far hanging upside down on a hook beside some other puppets. Peppino noticed that no two of the puppets looked the same and this caused him to wonder what *he* looked like. Towards the end of Peppino's first day a young girl, whom the puppet-maker called 'daughter', came to look at him. Of course, Peppino didn't know she was a young girl, but he did wonder why she was able to move about by herself, just like the puppet-maker. 'Daughter' took Peppino off his hook and laughed as she said, 'What a funny face you have, Peppino.' Then she laughed louder still. For some reason this hurt Peppino and he began to dislike his face, even though he had never seen it. Not long after this the lights went out and 'daughter' and the puppet-maker went away and all was quiet. Peppino was still thinking about his face when he heard a voice near him say, 'They have gone; we can do what we like now.' Peppino heard some shuffling sounds as it gradually began to get light again. He then saw that some of the puppets were now up the other way. While trying to see what they were doing Peppino found that he could move quite easily, so he crept over quietly and peeped at the puppets from behind a curtain.

[*Curtain up shows the Magician and the Clown on stage with Peppino peeping around the curtain at stage left.*]

BLINKIE: I wonder what the master is going to do with the new one?

MAGICIAN: Perhaps he is going to do something different. I must remember to look in my crystal ball.

[*He looks in Peppino's direction and nearly catches him, but Peppino dodges back just in time.*]

BLINKIE: Then he will be laying us aside and . . .

MAGICIAN: [*interrupting*] You don't have to worry; he always needs a clown in the show. As for me, I think I have earned a rest. After all I have been playing all the magician parts for years now.

[*Peppino continues to peek at them from time to time.*]

BLINKIE: Then who will be the magician? And you can't stop being the magician until you can remember how to turn the strong man back into himself again.

MAGICIAN: Yes, of course, that is a little unfortunate, but as soon as I remember the spell I will attend to it.

85

BLINKIE: The master is still wondering where Dumbello is. He would be angry if he knew you had turned him into a chair.

MAGICIAN: Dumbello was such a nuisance. I thought he needed sitting on. [*He catches sight of Peppino peering round the curtain.*] Ah, Peppino, come out here and let us have a good look at you.

[*Peppino goes hesitatingly to centre stage and the Magician and Clown look him over with interest.*]

MAGICIAN: Well, you look quite promising, yes, quite promising.

PEPPINO: Do I? I don't know what I look like.

BLINKIE: I'm glad you are not a clown.

MAGICIAN: [*turning to the clown*] Bring the mirror, Blinkie, and let Peppino see himself.

[*Clown exits stage right.*]

MAGICIAN: [*to Peppino*] Now you will soon know what you look like. [*Clown enters stage right with property mirror which is on a stand.*] Ah, here is the mirror.

[*The clown stands the mirror on the playboard right of centre stage and facing upstage. Peppino crosses to the mirror and looks into it. He jumps back a little as though startled and then leans forward to peer into it. He then moves his head from side to side to satisfy himself that it is really he.*]

PEPPINO: [*still looking in the mirror*] Is that me? Is that what I look like?

MAGICIAN: Yes, Peppino, that is you. Don't you like you?

[*Peppino looks at the Magician and then back to the mirror as the Clown exits stage right.*]

PEPPINO: [*shaking his head*] No!

MAGICIAN: That is the way you were made, so you will have to put up with it.

[*Peppino looks at the mirror again and then at the Magician.*]

PEPPINO: I heard you say, sir, that you were the magician. Could you change my face for me?

MAGICIAN: Change your face! Why do you want to change it, and what do you want to be?

PEPPINO: [*slowly*] I think I would like to be like — like 'daughter'.

MAGICIAN: [*surprised*] Like 'daughter'! But 'daughter' is a girl — and a human being.

PEPPINO: Why can't I look like a human being?

MAGICIAN: But you are a puppet. You have character. Why would you want to look like a human being?

PEPPINO: 'Daughter' laughed at me when she saw me. She seemed to think I had a funny face.

MAGICIAN: That isn't anything to be ashamed of — lots of puppets have funny faces. Sometimes I wish I had a funny face. The audience likes a funny face.

PEPPINO: But I don't like to be laughed at.

MAGICIAN: You won't be so sensitive about it after you have done a few shows.

PEPPINO: I still don't want to be laughed at. Please change me to look like a human being.

MAGICIAN: All right, Peppino, if you really want me to. [*He turns and addresses the audience.*] After all, this sort of thing keeps me in practice. [*He looks around him.*] Now, where is Blinkie? He must bring my magic screen.

[*The Magician goes to each side of the stage in turn and calls 'Blinkie'. During this time Peppino is stealing glances at himself in the mirror. He then picks the mirror up and puts it down again in a similar position at stage left. He looks in it again as though moving it will have some effect on what he sees. Blinkie now enters from stage right.*]

MAGICIAN: [*seeing Blinkie*] Ah, there you are Blinkie. Will you bring me my magic screen? Peppino wants a different face.

BLINKIE: A different face! Does he know you can't remember how to turn the chair back into the strong man?

MAGICIAN: [*in stage whisper and with hand raised to lips*] Sh-h-h-h. This will give me some practice. Please bring the screen.

[*Blinkie shakes his head slowly and exits stage right.*]

MAGICIAN: [*looking at Peppino*] Now, let me see, let me see. I will give you a head like a human boy. What do you think of that?

PEPPINO: [*as Blinkie enters stage right with the screen*] That will be wonderful, then nobody will laugh at me.

BLINKIE: [*struggling with the screen*] I wouldn't be too sure if I were you.

MAGICIAN: [*ignoring the remark*] Let me think for a moment. [*He moves about the stage mumbling a jumble of spells.*] No, no, that would make you an alligator.

PEPPINO: I don't want to be an alligator; I want to be a human boy.

BLINKIE: [*who is resting the screen on the playboard at stage right*] I hope you are lucky, that's all!

MAGICIAN: Ah, ha, I have it! Blinkie. Hold up the screen and you, Peppino, must go behind it while I say the spell.

[*Blinkie picks up the screen and holds it up at centre stage with his back to the audience.*]

MAGICIAN: [*turning to Peppino*] You must go behind the screen now, Peppino, and come out when I have pronounced the spell.

[*Peppino goes behind the screen, but looks out once or twice, as though a bit apprehensive, while the Magician is still thinking about his spell. At this point the dog's head should be ready to put on the finger the moment Peppino's own head is removed.*]

MAGICIAN: [*suddenly*] I think I have it! Ready Peppino? [*He begins to recite a spell.*] Ippi kaki — Winni waki — count to . . . .

BLINKIE: [*interrupting*] No, no, no, that is the one you used on the strong man!

MAGICIAN: [*mildly*] Oh, is it? Then I must think again.

[*He moves around tapping his forehead as though thinking deeply. Peppino looks cautiously out from behind the screen, but ducks back again as the Magician says suddenly.*]

MAGICIAN: Now I have it! It was just the wrong way round last time.

[*He begins the spell again.*] Winni waki — ippi kaki — count to one and out you come — there!

PEPPINO: [*from behind screen*] One!

[*Peppino comes out from behind the screen to stage left. He has on the dog's head with red hair.*]

BLINKIE: [*lowering the screen a little*] What have you done now? The spell is wrong again!

[*Peppino looks in the mirror, which is still standing on the playboard at stage left, and jumps back. He then begins to bark at the reflection. The Magician looks closely at Peppino and pats him on the head.*]

MAGICIAN: It does look like it, doesn't it? [*to Peppino*] Nice dog. Now, now, now, don't worry, I must have used the wrong spell. We'll soon put it right. [*He turns to the audience.*] This is what happens when you have to stick to a script for so long — you forget your own spells.

[*The Magician turns to Peppino and pats his head again, at which Peppino growls.*]

MAGICIAN: Go behind the screen and we'll put this right.

BLINKIE: [*to the audience*] It is more likely that I will have to go for some dog biscuit.

88

[*Peppino moves towards the screen, but stops to nuzzle the clown's face. The clown backs away, still holding the screen.*]

BLINKIE: Down, down, good dog, good dog. Behind here, behind the screen. [*He holds the screen in place and Peppino obediently goes behind it.*]

MAGICIAN: If that spell wasn't right, it must be this one. [*He begins to chant.*] Hoo-do, Voo-do, what would you do? Count to three, then look at me.

[*Peppino barks three times and then comes out from the screen to stage left. This time he has the cannibal's head, with red hair. The clown lets out a frightened yell and backs away to stage right. He keeps the screen between himself and Peppino, who is executing a kind of war dance.*]

MAGICIAN: Gracious me, wrong again! [*He goes up to Peppino.*] Are you sure you want to be a human boy, Peppino? Wouldn't you like to stay as you were?

PEPPINO: [*in unintelligible language and nodding his head.*] Ha-a-a-a, gulpp, koomph, wha-a-a-a . . .

MAGICIAN: [*interrupting*] You said wha-a?

PEPPINO: Ya-ah!

MAGICIAN: Good, that will not take long. I'll soon have you looking like yourself again, but you must go behind the screen. [*He notices Blinkie still hiding behind the screen at stage right.*] Blinkie, bring the screen out here. [*Blinkie moves cautiously to centre stage with the screen. Peppino goes behind it, but he suddenly pops his head over the top. Blinkie lets out a cry and nearly drops the screen.*]

MAGICIAN: [*by now confused and a little agitated*] Let me see, let me see, where was I? Winni waki — ippi kaki [*The dog's head is poked around the screen.*] No, no, Hoo-do, Voo-do . . . [*The dog's head disappears and is replaced by the cannibal's head.*] Oh dear, why can't I get it right? Voo-do, waki . . . [*Cannibal's head reappears, quickly followed by the dog's head on the other side of the screen.*]

MAGICIAN: Oh-h, I do seem to be thoroughly confused. [*He turns to the audience.*] How am I going to make Peppino right again if I can't remember the spell? He is the master's newest puppet and he will not be pleased at all . . .

BLINKIE: [*still holding the screen*] Do hurry up and remember the spell. I can't hold the screen up much longer.

MAGICIAN: I really thought I knew it well,
How to make and break a spell;
But it seems it is beyond me.
Nothing works, not even metamorphorosomi.

[*At the word 'metamorphorosomi' Peppino comes out from behind the screen, himself again.*]

MAGICIAN: [*delighted*] Ah, that is it, METAMORPHOROSOMI [*He says this loudly. Blinkie lowers the screen and staggers with it off stage right.*]

MAGICIAN: Fancy me forgetting a simple word like that. Now, Peppino, since I remember the spell, would you like me to try again?

PEPPINO: No, no, thank you, I feel quite all right as I am. [*He looks in the mirror, still at stage left.*] I don't look so bad, do I?

MAGICIAN: Of course not. I couldn't really understand why you wanted to look like a human being instead of a puppet. Do you know that, if you looked like a human being and had to act like a puppet, you would be quite ridiculous, which is much worse than being funny. But, if you want me to, I . . .

PEPPINO: [*hurriedly interrupting*] I think I'll stay the way I am, thank you very much. I'm sure I'll get used ot it.

BLINKIE: [*entering in a state of excitement from stage right*] The strong man is the strong man again! When you shouted the spell word he changed back to himself and now he is looking for you.

MAGICIAN: [*rather hurriedly*] Well now, I really think it is time for us all to return to our hooks. The master will be back again soon and it would never do if he found us out here. Come along, come along.

[*He ushers them off to stage left as the lights dim and the curtain closes.*]